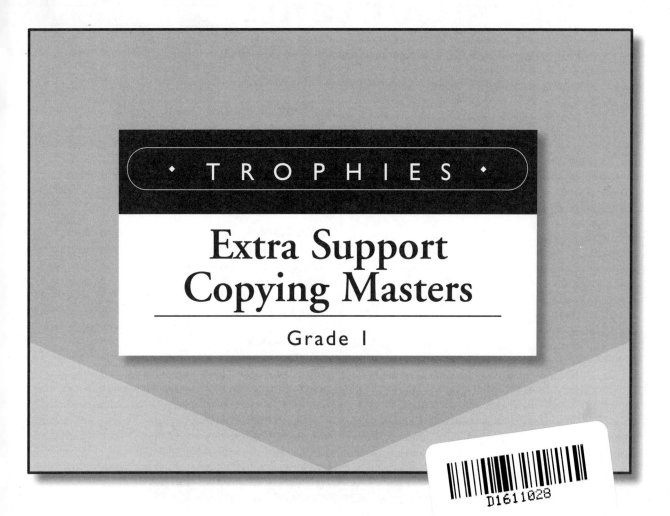

· TROPHIES ·

Extra Support
Copying Masters

Grade 1

Harcourt

Orlando   Boston   Dallas   Chicago   San Diego

Visit *The Learning Site!*
www.harcourtschool.com

ISBN 0-15-323506-3

9 10 018 10 09 08 07 06 05 04

Contents

GUESS WHO – LEVEL 1

CATCH A DREAM – LEVEL 2

Contents

HERE AND THERE – LEVEL 3

TIME TOGETHER – LEVEL 4

Contents

· TROPHIES ·

Level One

Guess Who

Name _____

▶ **Say the name of each picture. Circle the pictures that have the sound /a/.**

1.

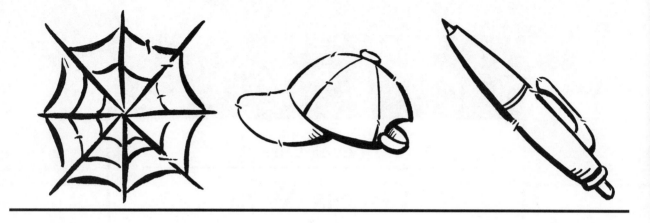

2.

3.

SCHOOL-HOME CONNECTION Ask your child to say the name of each picture whose name has the short *a* sound as in *at*.

9

Extra Support
Guess Who • Lesson 1

© Harcourt

▶ **Say the name of the first picture in each row. Color the picture whose name rhymes with it.**

1.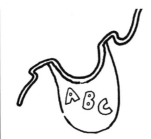

2.

3.    10

4.

5.

SCHOOL-HOME CONNECTION Have your child say each pair of rhyming words. Then ask your child to think of more pairs of rhyming words.

11

Extra Support
Guess Who • Lesson 1

▶ **Look at each picture. Read each
sentence. Trace the word that completes
the sentence.**

1. I look ____ up ____ .

2. I look ____ down ____ .

3. I ____ got ____ a bat.

 TRY THIS! Draw a big kite. Write about your picture.

SCHOOL-HOME CONNECTION Read the
sentences with your child. Ask your child to
tell you what is happening in each picture.

12

Extra Support
Guess Who • Lesson 1

▶ **Look at each picture. Read each sentence. Trace the word that completes the sentence.**

1. I am a __cat__.

2. I am __Max__.

3. Max has a __cap__.

4. I am a __bat__.

5. I __am__ Jan.

SCHOOL-HOME CONNECTION Write *am*, *Jan*, and *bat* on a sheet of paper. Invite your child to trace the letters you wrote.

Extra Support
Guess Who • Lesson 1

Name _____

▶ **Write 1, 2, and 3 to put the pictures in order.**

1.

_____   _____   _____

- - - - -   - - - - -   - - - - -

_____   _____   _____

2.

_____   _____   _____

- - - - -   - - - - -   - - - - -

_____   _____   _____

3.

_____   _____   _____

- - - - -   - - - - -   - - - - -

_____   _____   _____

SCHOOL-HOME CONNECTION Have your
child tell about a group of pictures on this
page. Ask: *What happens first? What happens next?
What happens last?*

14

Extra Support
Guess Who • Lesson 1

© Harcourt

Name _____

▶ **Say the name of each picture. If the name rhymes with <u>tap</u>, circle <u>ap</u>. If the name rhymes with <u>sat</u>, circle <u>at</u>.**

1.

at   ap

2.

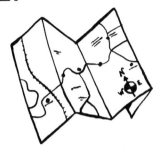

at   ap

3.

at   ap

4.

at   ap

5.

at   ap

6.

at   ap

7.

at   ap

8.

at   ap

9.

at   ap

© Harcourt

SCHOOL-HOME CONNECTION Ask your child to point to all pictures whose names end with *at*. Then ask your child to point to all pictures whose names end with *ap*.

15

Extra Support
Guess Who • Lesson 1

Name _____

▶ **Color each picture whose name has the vowel sound /a/ as in <u>at</u>.**

1.

2.

3.

4.

5.

6.

7.

8.

 SCHOOL-HOME CONNECTION Ask your child to point to all the pictures that have the short *a* sound as in *at*. Then have your child practice writing the letter *a*.

 17

Extra Support
Guess Who • Lesson 2

© Harcourt

Name _____

▶ **Trace the words that have the sound /a/.**
Circle the letter that stands for the sound
/a/ in each word.

1.

hat

2.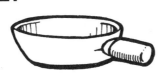

pan

3.

cat

4.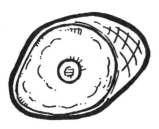

ham

5.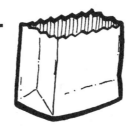

bag

6.

jam

7.

fan

8.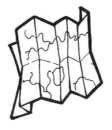

map

9.

cap

© Harcourt

SCHOOL-HOME CONNECTION Write the
words *map, bag,* and *ham.* Ask your child to point
to the letter in each word that stands
for the /a/ sound.

Extra Support
Guess Who • Lesson 2

Name _____

► **Look at each picture. Read each sentence. Trace the word that completes the sentence.**

1. Jan ___and___ Max ran.

2. Max ran ___in___.

3. Can Jan go ___in___?

4. ___Yes___, Jan can go in!

5. ___Oh___, Jan!

 TRY THIS Say a sentence about Jan and Max. Use a word you traced.

 SCHOOL-HOME CONNECTION Read the sentences with your child. Ask your child to read the words he or she traced and tell you what is happening in each picture.

20

Extra Support
Guess Who • Lesson 2

Name _____

▶ **Say the name of each picture. Then trace the word.**

1.

hat

2.

sand

3.

bat

4.

band

5.

lamp

6.

fan

SCHOOL-HOME CONNECTION Write *band, bat,* and *sand* on a sheet of paper. Invite your child to trace the letters you wrote. Ask your child to draw a picture of sand on a beach.

21

Extra Support
Guess Who • Lesson 2

© Harcourt

▶ **The letter s has been added to some words below. Trace the words that have the s ending.**

come
_____

1. Pam ___comes___ in.

pat
_____

2. Pam ___pats___ Rags.

cat
_____

3. A ___cat___ comes.

look
_____

4. A cat ___looks___ at Rags.

SCHOOL-HOME CONNECTION Write the words *pan* and *pans*. Have your child tell you how these words are different. Ask your child to draw a picture of one pan and a picture of two pans.

22

Extra Support
Guess Who • Lesson 2

© Harcourt

▶ **Say the name of each picture. Two picture names in each row have the vowel sound /i/. Circle and color the pictures whose names have the vowel sound /i/.**

1.

2.

3.

SCHOOL-HOME CONNECTION Have your child say the name of each picture that has the vowel sound /i/, as in *pin*.

24

© Harcourt

Name _____

▶ **Say the name of the first picture in each row. Circle and color the picture in each row whose name rhymes with it.**

1.			
tree	bat	pig	bathtub

2.			
lip	zipper	mop	cat

3.			
man	welcome mat	peanut	pin

4.			
bib	pan	crib	dog

5.			
dish	box	top	fish

SCHOOL-HOME CONNECTION Have your child say each pair of rhyming words. Then ask your child to say other words that rhyme with the pair.

26

Name _____

▶ **Read each sentence. Trace the word that completes the sentence.**

1. Jim and Jill ______ up a hill.

2. ___They___ walk in sand.

3. Jim and Jill ___make___ a six.

TRY THIS! Make a big six. Draw six things next to it.

SCHOOL-HOME CONNECTION Write *walk*, *they*, and *make* on a sheet of paper. Have your child say a sentence using each word.

Extra Support
Guess Who • Lesson 3

▶ **Circle the words on the bib that have the vowel sound /i/.**

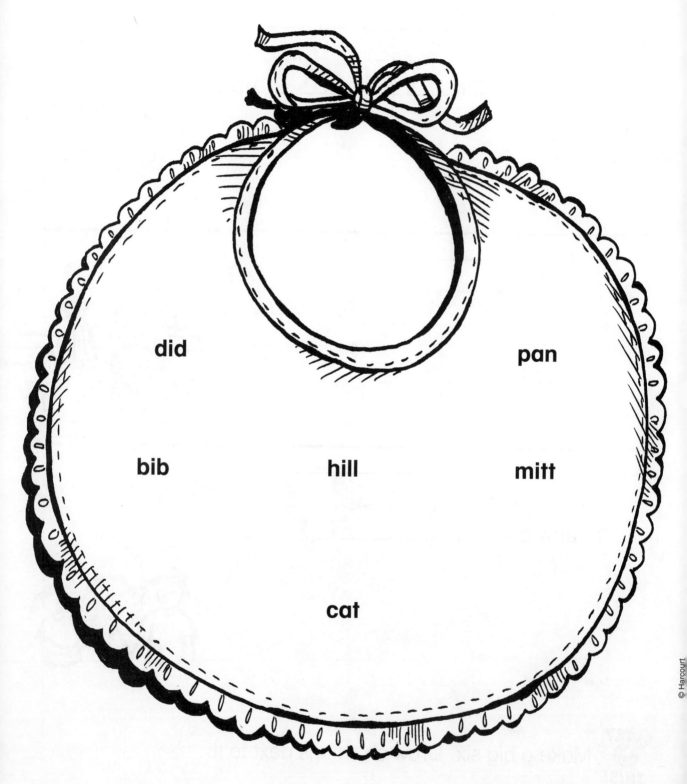

did

pan

bib

hill

mitt

cat

SCHOOL-HOME CONNECTION Have your child read aloud three words that have the vowel sound /i/, as in *bib*.

28

Extra Support
Guess Who • Lesson 3

© Harcourt

Name _____

▶ **Look at the top picture. Draw the balls**
   and cat where they go in the picture below.

SCHOOL-HOME CONNECTION Have your
child tell you about what she or he drew at the
bottom of the page.

Extra Support
Guess Who • Lesson 3

Name _____

▶ **Trace the contraction that completes each sentence.**

Here is

1. Here's the bag.

What is

2. What's in it?

It is

3. It's a cat.

Pat is

4. Pat's the cat.

SCHOOL-HOME CONNECTION Have your child choose two contractions and point to the apostrophe and *s* at the end of each. Then ask what two words each contraction stands for.

30

Extra Support
Guess Who • Lesson 3

© Harcourt

Name _____

▶ **Say the name of each picture. One picture name in each row ends with the sound /k/. Circle the pictures whose names end with the sound /k/.**

1.

2.

3.

SCHOOL-HOME CONNECTION Have your child say the name of each circled picture. Then ask what sound she or he hears at the very end of the word.

32

Extra Support
Guess Who • Lesson 4

© Harcourt

▶ **Trace the words on the sack that end with the sound /k/.**

sick

pick   sack

cap

tack   ten

SCHOOL-HOME CONNECTION Have your child choose three words that end in ck to read to you. Ask your child to tell the ending sound of each word (/k/ as in *sack*).

Extra Support
Guess Who • Lesson 4

Name _____

▶ **Look at each picture. Draw a line from the blank to the word that completes the sentence.**

want   it

1. Do you _____to go?

a   now

2. Yes, I want to go _____.

we   too

3. Oh, no! It's _____ big.

help   cup

4. I can _____.

are   play

5. We can go and _____.

© Harcourt

SCHOOL-HOME CONNECTION Read each sentence with your child. Have your child tell you why he or she chose that word.

35

▶ **Circle each picture name. Then trace the word.**

1.

tack

Rick

tack

2.

sack

kick

kick

3.

pack

sick

sick

4.

sack

chick

sack

SCHOOL-HOME CONNECTION Ask your child to read aloud the words he or she traced. Ask what is the same in all the words. (They end with *ck*.)

Extra Support
Guess Who • Lesson 4

© Harcourt

Name _____

▶ **Write 1, 2, and 3 to put the pictures in order.**

_____   _____   _____

- - - - - - - - -   - - - - - - - - -   - - - - - - - - -

_____   _____   _____

_____   _____   _____

- - - - - - - - -   - - - - - - - - -   - - - - - - - - -

_____   _____   _____

SCHOOL-HOME CONNECTION Have your child choose a set of pictures on this page. Ask your child to use the words *first*, *next*, and *last* to tell you what is happening in the pictures.

37

Extra Support
Guess Who • Lesson 4

© Harcourt

Name _____

▶ **Look at the two words above the sentence. Then trace the contraction that finishes each sentence.**

I will

1. _____I'll_____ sit at camp.

You will

2. _____You'll_____ dig at camp.

---

we will

3. Now _____we'll_____ play at camp.

SCHOOL-HOME CONNECTION Read the sentences with your child. Ask your child to tell the two words that go together to make the contractions.

38

Extra Support
Guess Who • Lesson 4

© Harcourt

▶ **Say the name of each picture. Trace the letter o to complete each word. Then color the picture.**

1.

dog

2.

top

3.

box

4.

mop

5.

pot

6.
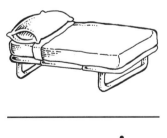
cot

SCHOOL-HOME CONNECTION Have your child choose two words from the page. Ask which vowel sound each word has. Have your child read and trace the words.

40

Extra Support
Guess Who • Lesson 5

Name _____

▶ **Say the name of the first picture in each row. Circle and color the picture whose name rhymes with it.**

1.    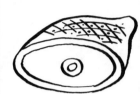      

2.    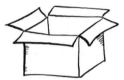      

3.          

4.          

5.          

SCHOOL-HOME CONNECTION Have your child say a pair of rhyming words from the page. Ask your child to write the vowel in each word: *o*.

Extra Support
Guess Who • Lesson 5

© Harcourt

► **Look at each picture. Draw a line from
the blank to the word that completes
each sentence. Then write the word.**

so   we

_____

- - - - - - - - - - -

1. The pack is _____ big!

go   of

_____

- - - - - - - - - - -

2. The pack is on the back _____
the cat.

A   Don't

_____

- - - - - - - - - - -

3. Oh! _____ back up!

SCHOOL-HOME CONNECTION Have your child
read each word he or she used to complete a
sentence, and then tell you about the story.

43

Extra Support
Guess Who • Lesson 5

▶ Say the name of each picture. Circle the letter that stands for the vowel sound in each picture name.

1.

o   i

2.

o   i

3.

o   i

4.

o   i

5.

o   i

6.

o   i

SCHOOL-HOME CONNECTION Have your child say each picture name and tell why he or she circled each letter.

Extra Support
Guess Who • Lesson 5

Name _____

▶ **Look at the word and the ending. Then
trace the new word that finishes each sentence.**

look + ed

1. I <u>looked</u> at you.

look + ing

2. Now you are <u>looking</u>
at me.

pick + ed

3. I <u>picked</u> up a box.

pick + ing

4. Now you are <u>picking</u>
one up.

SCHOOL-HOME CONNECTION Have your child
read aloud one of the completed sentences. Ask
how he or she changed the word above the line
to complete the sentence.

45

Extra Support
Guess Who • Lesson 5

Name _____

▶ **Circle each word that ends with <u>all</u>. Then trace the word.**

1. My dog is not ____ 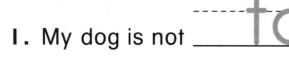 tall ____.

2. My dog is in the ____ hall ____.

3. I can ____ call ____ my dog.

4. My dog wants to play ____ ball ____.

SCHOOL-HOME CONNECTION Have your child read each circled word. Ask him or her about the story on this page. Then ask your child to write the word *all*.

Extra Support
Guess Who • Lesson 6

© Harcourt

Name _____

▶ **Cut out the words. Paste the words that end in <u>all</u> on the ball.**

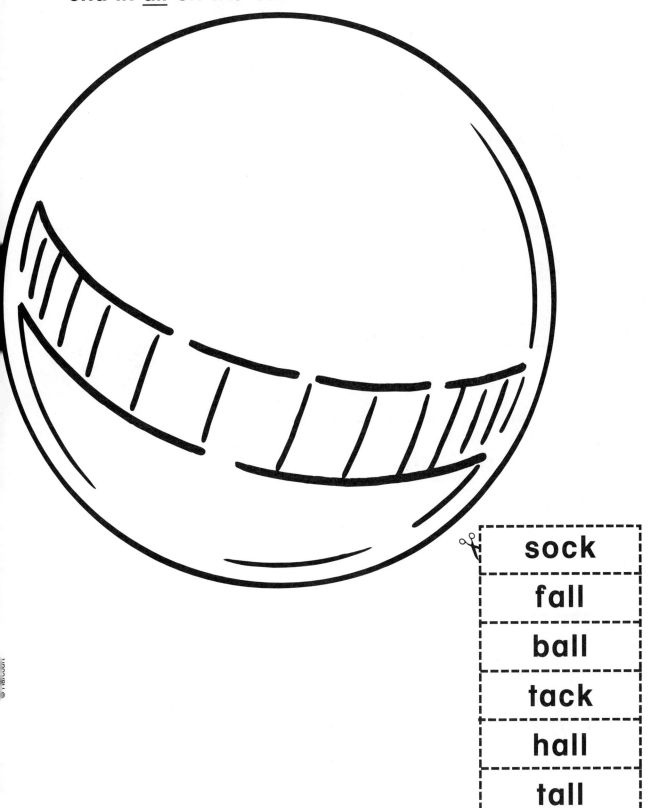

| sock |
| fall |
| ball |
| tack |
| hall |
| tall |

SCHOOL-HOME CONNECTION Have your child choose three words from the page to read to you. Ask your child to say the ending sound of each word.

49

Extra Support
Guess Who • Lesson 6

Name _____

► **Circle the word that completes each sentence.**

buy   my

1. We can _____ the little dog.

Do   Where

2. _____ is it?

are   that

3. It's _____ one.

my   very

4. It's _____ fast.

SCHOOL-HOME CONNECTION Have your
child read some of the sentences aloud. Ask
why the circled words make sense in the
sentences.

50

Extra Support
Guess Who • Lesson 6

© Harcourt

Name _____

▶ **Say the name of the first picture in each row. Circle the picture whose name rhymes with it.**

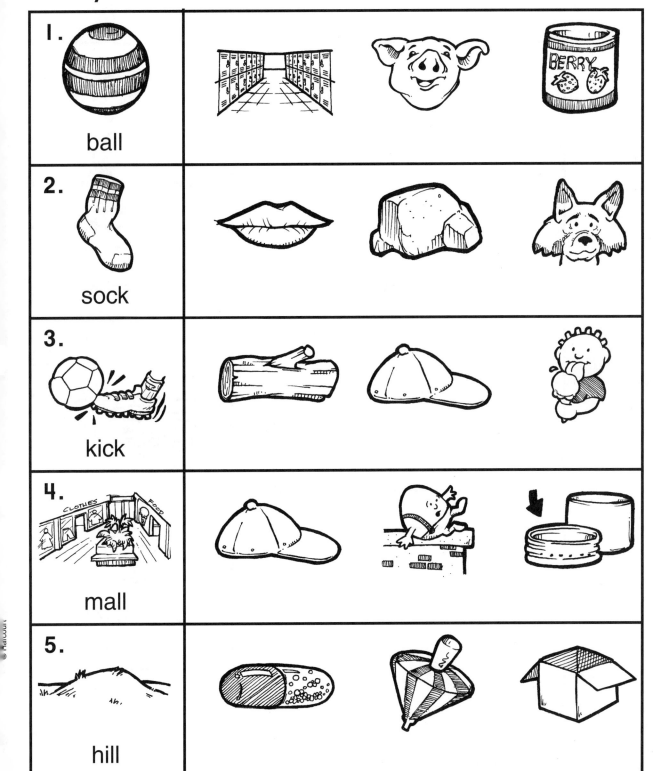

1. ball

2. sock

3. kick

4. mall

5. hill

SCHOOL-HOME CONNECTION Ask your child to tell you the rhyming words in each row.

51

Extra Support
Guess Who • Lesson 6

Name _____

▶ **Cut out the pictures. Then paste them in the correct order.**

1.

2.

3.

SCHOOL-HOME CONNECTION Have your child tell how she or he knew which order to use for the pictures. Encourage your child to use the words *first*, *next*, and *last*.

52

Extra Support
Guess Who • Lesson 6

© Harcourt

Name _____

▶ **Look at each picture. Read the sentence.**
  Trace the contraction that stands for the
  underlined words.

<u>**is**</u> + <u>**not**</u>

1. Pam ___isn't___ here.

<u>**do**</u> + <u>**not**</u>

2. I ___don't___ see Jan and Rick.

<u>**are**</u> + <u>**not**</u>

3. They ___aren't___ here.

<u>**Did**</u> + <u>**not**</u>

4. ___Didn't___ they come?

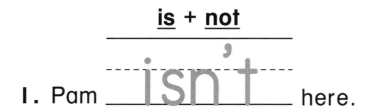

SCHOOL-HOME CONNECTION Have your
child tell how the words above the lines
changed. Ask which letter the apostrophe
took the place of in each word (*o*). Invite your child to
talk about what is happening on the page.

53

Extra Support
Guess Who • Lesson 6

Level Two

Catch a Dream

Name _____

▶ **Say each picture name. Circle and color the pictures whose names have the same vowel sound as the word <u>bed</u>.**

1. 	2. 	3. 
4. 	5. 	6. 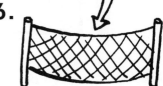
7. 	8. 	9. 
10. 	11. 	12. 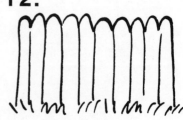

SCHOOL-HOME CONNECTION With your child, say all the picture names on the page. Then have your child say the picture names that contain the short *e* sound.

3

Extra Support
Catch a Dream • Lesson 1

© Harcourt

Name _____

▶ **Say each picture name. Circle and color the picture whose name has the vowel sound /e/ as in <u>bed</u>.**

1.

2.

3.

4.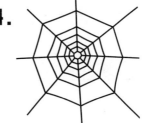

5.

6.

7.

8.

SCHOOL-HOME CONNECTION Ask your child to point to all of the pictures that have the short *e* sound as in *bed*. Then have your child practice writing the letter *e*.

5

Extra Support
Catch a Dream • Lesson 1

Name _____

▶ **Look at each picture and read the sentence. Trace the word or words that complete the sentence.**

1. The cat ___with___ Meg is ___her___ pet.

2. The cat ___was___ sick.

3. The vet ___said___ to let the cat rest.

4. The cat rests ___every day___ .

SCHOOL-HOME CONNECTION Read the sentences with your child. Talk about the meanings of the words your child traced.

◆ **6**

© Harcourt

Extra Support
Catch a Dream • Lesson 1

Name _____

▶ **Look at each picture. Circle the word that matches the picture.**

1.

jet

job

2.

dig

doll

3.

peck

pond

4.

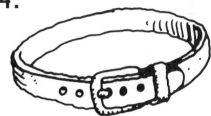

belt

boss

5.

cot

cat

6.

wet

wall

7.

fan

fox

8.

milk

mend

© Harcourt

SCHOOL-HOME CONNECTION Ask your child to read aloud the words he or she circled. Talk about the letter *o* in some words, and the /o/ sound it stands for.

7

Extra Support
Catch a Dream • Lesson 1

Name _____

▶ **Read the sentences. Circle the picture
that shows the place where the sentences
could happen.**

1. The ball went down the hill.
Tom ran to get the ball.
Mom and Dan ran to get the ball.

2. Let's go to bed now.
Mom will come up.
You can go on top today.

SCHOOL-HOME CONNECTION Ask your child how
she or he knew which picture to circle. Then take
turns choosing pictures on the page and saying
something that could happen in that setting.

8

Extra Support
Catch a Dream • Lesson 1

© Harcourt

Name _____

▶ **Say the name of each picture. Listen to the beginning sounds. Trace the two letters that stand for the beginning sounds.**

1.    sp   st

2.    st   sn

3.    sl   sk

4.    sn   st

5.    sp   sn

6.    sk   sl

© Harcourt

SCHOOL-HOME CONNECTION With your child, name words that begin with each of the following letter pairs: *sp, sn, sl, st,* and *sk.*

9

Extra Support
Catch a Dream • Lesson 1

Name _____

▶ **Say the name of each picture. Circle and color the picture whose name begins or ends with *th*.**

1.

2.

3.

4.

5.

6.

7.

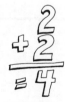 

8.

SCHOOL-HOME CONNECTION Say the following words and ask your child to say a rhyming word that begins with the sound *th*: *hem* (them), *bin* (thin), *sink* (think), and *bank* (thank).

11

Extra Support
Catch a Dream • Lesson 2

© Harcourt

▶ **Trace the word. Draw a line to the picture that matches it.**

SCHOOL-HOME CONNECTION Ask your child to name five words that begin or end with *th*.

◀13▶

Extra Support
Catch a Dream • Lesson 2

© Harcourt

Name _____

▶ **Look at each picture. Read the sentence. Trace the word or words that complete the sentence.**

1. _____ She _____ has _____ friends _____.

2. They _____ could _____ _____ use _____ his help.

3. Help me _____ put _____ it here.

4. Look! A _____ new _____ hat.

SCHOOL-HOME CONNECTION Ask your child to make up different sentences using the words *she, could, use, put, friends,* and *new.*

Extra Support
Catch a Dream • Lesson 2

© Harcourt

Name _____

▶ **Say each picture name. Circle and color the two pictures in each row whose names have the same vowel sound.**

1.

2.

3.

4.

5.

SCHOOL-HOME CONNECTION Ask your child to explain why he or she circled each pair of pictures.

 15

Extra Support
Catch a Dream • Lesson 2

Name _____

► **Read the words at the top of the chart.**
Write the words from the box where they belong on
the chart.

tent	nest	best	dent

 _____ vest _____

 _____ bent

 _____

 _____

 _____

 _____

SCHOOL-HOME CONNECTION Ask your child to
read the words he or she wrote in each column. Then
ask your child to make up a sentence that uses a
word with *-est* and one that uses a word with *-ent*.

16

Extra Support
Catch a Dream • Lesson 2

Name _____

▶ **Say the name of each picture. Circle and color the picture whose name has the vowel sound /u/, as in <u>cup</u>.**

1.

2.

3.

4.

5.

6.

7.

8.

 SCHOOL-HOME CONNECTION Ask your child to point to all the pictures that have the short *u* sound, as in *cup*. Then have your child practice writing the letter *u* in words.

 18

Extra Support
Catch a Dream • Lesson 3

Name _____

▶ **Say the names of the pictures. Circle and color the two pictures in each row whose names rhyme.**

1.

2.

  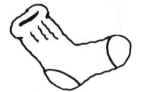 

3.

4.

5.

20

Extra Support
Catch a Dream • Lesson 3

© Harcourt

Name _____

▶ **Look at each picture and read each sentence. Trace the words that complete each sentence.**

1. _____ **Your** pup is _____ **out**.

2. Mom _____ **says he** _____ must rest.

3. Dan _____ **gives** the pup a

hug at _____ **night**.

4. _____ **People** come

_____ **when** the pup is up.

SCHOOL-HOME CONNECTION Read the sentences with your child. Talk about how the sentences match the pictures.

Extra Support
Catch a Dream • Lesson 3

© Harcourt

Name _____

▶ **Say the picture names. Circle and color the picture in each row whose name rhymes with the first picture in the row.**

1.			

2.			

3.			

4.			

SCHOOL-HOME CONNECTION Have your
child say each pair of rhyming words. Then ask
him or her to think of more pairs of rhyming
words that use the vowel *e* as in *pet*, the vowel *u*
as in *cup*, and the digraph *ck* as in *chick*.

Extra Support
Catch a Dream • Lesson 3

© Harcourt

Name _____

▶ **Say the picture names. Circle the two pictures in each row whose names start with the same sounds.**

I.

2.

3.

4.

5.

 23

Extra Support
Catch a Dream • Lesson 3

Name _____

▶ **Say each picture name. Circle the picture if its name ends with ng.**

1.

2.

3.

4.

5.

6.
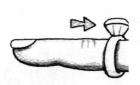 

7.

8.

SCHOOL-HOME CONNECTION Ask your child to point to all the pictures whose names end with *ng*.

25

Extra Support
Catch a Dream • Lesson 4

Name _____

 Say the name of the first picture in each
row. Circle the picture in the row whose name
rhymes with the first picture name.

1.       

2.          

3.    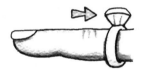   

4.          

5.          

SCHOOL-HOME CONNECTION Have your
child say each pair of rhyming words. Then ask
him or her to think of more pairs of rhyming
words that end with *ng*.

27

Extra Support
Catch a Dream • Lesson 4

Phonics
Diphthong:
/ng/ ng

Name _____

▶ **Look at each picture and read each sentence. Trace the word or words that complete each sentence.**

1. Bob has ___two___ frogs.

2. A frog ___grows___ if it

   can ___eat___ well.

3. Bob got his frogs

   ___from___ a pond.

4. Are the frogs ___gone___

   ___or___ not?

SCHOOL-HOME CONNECTION Read the sentences with your child. Talk about how the sentences go with the pictures.

◆28◆

Extra Support
Catch a Dream • Lesson 4

▶ **Look at each picture. Trace the word that names it.**

1.
sled

2.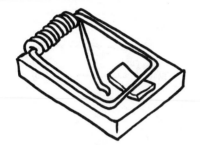
trap

3.
stand

4.
stamp

5.
sing

Name _____

▶ **Look at the big picture. Circle the little pictures that show things in the big picture. Then trace the names of pictures you circled.**

---

1.  tent

2.  dog

3.  hat

4.  cats

5.  log

6.  frog

 SCHOOL-HOME CONNECTION Have your child explain why he or she circled certain pictures and traced certain words. Ask your child about things he or she sees in the picture.

 30

Extra Support
Catch a Dream • Lesson 4

▶ **Look at each picture and read the sentence. Trace the word that completes the sentence.**

1. _____ He's _____ calling Bill.

2. Bill _____ isn't _____ picking up.

3. _____ He'll _____ go get Bill.

4. He _____ can't _____ see Bill.

5. _____ They'll _____ play with the ball.

SCHOOL-HOME CONNECTION Read the sentences with your child. Ask what two words make up the contractions your child traced.

31

Extra Support
Catch a Dream • Lesson 4

▶ **Listen as your teacher names the pictures. Circle and color the two pictures in each row whose names rhyme.**

I.

| thorn | zebra | dog | corn |

2.

| banana | fork | stork | fish |

3.

| snore | rainbow | store | jug |

4.

| tent | port | fan | short |

5.

| horn | pot | penny | torn |

SCHOOL-HOME CONNECTION Ask your child to say the picture names that rhyme. With your child, think of another word that rhymes with each pair.

33

Extra Support
Catch a Dream • Lesson 5

Name _____

▶ **Say each picture name. Circle and color the picture whose name has the same vowel sound as <u>sort</u>.**

sort

1.

2.

3.

4.

5.

6.

 SCHOOL-HOME CONNECTION Ask your child to point to all the pictures that have the /or/ sound as in *sort*. Then have your child practice writing the letters *or*.

Extra Support
Catch a Dream • Lesson 5

Name _____

► **Look at each picture and read the sentence. Trace the words that complete the sentence.**

1.  We _____ **need** _____ to _____ **be** _____ fast.

2.  I will _____ **try** _____ hard to run in a _____ **good** _____ time.

3.  It was _____ **our** _____ **time** _____ to win.

4.  "We _____ **saw** _____ you run _____ **right** _____ to the end!"

 SCHOOL-HOME CONNECTION Read the sentences with your child. Talk about how the sentences tell what is happening in the picture.

 36

Extra Support
Catch a Dream • Lesson 5

Name _____

▶ **Read each sentence. Trace the word that completes the sentence.**

1. This is ___for___ you.

2. The ___cord___ is off.

3. It is ___torn___.

4. It is a ___horn___.

5. They eat some ___corn___.

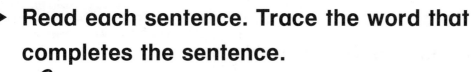

SCHOOL-HOME CONNECTION Read the sentences with your child. Talk about the vowel sound in each word he or she traced.

Extra Support
Catch a Dream • Lesson 5

▶ **Read the story beginning. Then trace the words that complete the sentences.**

One day, Dennis called his dog Tug. Tug did not come.
"Mom!" said Dennis. "Where is Tug?"
"Tug is not here," said Mom. "Ask Dad."
"Dad!" said Dennis. "Where is Tug?"
"Tug is not here," said Dad. "Let's look for Tug."
Dennis and Dad went out to look.

1. The story is mostly about .

2. Two more story characters are Mom

and .

 SCHOOL-HOME CONNECTION Have your child tell you about the story beginning. Invite her or him to read aloud the two sentences. Then ask what your child thinks might happen in the rest of the story.

38

Extra Support
Catch a Dream • Lesson 5

Name _____

▶ **Look at each picture. Read the sentence.**
   Trace the word that completes the sentence.

1. They play __softball__.

2. Norris has a __backpack__.

3. They play until __sunset__.

4. Mort is in the __bathtub__.

5. Doris likes __popcorn__.

SCHOOL-HOME CONNECTION Read the sentences with your child. Talk about the sentences and the pictures. Help your child make a list of other compound words, such as *anthill*, *playpen*, and *sandbox*.

Extra Support
Catch a Dream • Lesson 5

▶ **Say the name of each picture. Circle and color the picture whose name has the /sh/ sound as in <u>fish</u>**

1.

2.

3.

4.

 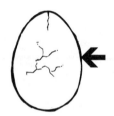

5.

 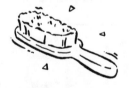

6.

7.

8.

SCHOOL-HOME CONNECTION Ask your child to point to all of the pictures that have the /sh/ sound, as in *shell*.

41

Extra Support
Catch a Dream • Lesson 6

▶ **Say the names of the pictures. Circle the two pictures in each row whose names have the /sh/ sound as in *fish*.**

1.

2.

3.

4.

 SCHOOL-HOME CONNECTION Ask your child to say the word that each picture represents. Help your child think of other words with the /sh/ sound.

 43

Extra Support
Catch a Dream • Lesson 6

Name _____

▶ **Look at each picture and read the sentence. Trace the word or words that complete the sentence.**

1. I got ___some___ new fish.

2. ___How many___ did you get?

3. Some ___hide___ to get ___away___ from big fish.

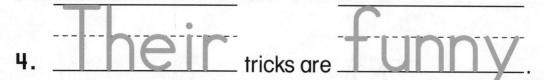

4. ___Their___ tricks are ___funny___.

SCHOOL-HOME CONNECTION Read the sentences with your child. Talk about how the sentences go with the pictures. Help your child make up more sentences with the new words.

44

Name _____

► **Look at each picture. Trace the word that names the picture.**

1.

fish   ship

2.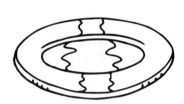

dish   shed

3.

rash   shut

4.

cash   rush

5.

mash   wish

SCHOOL-HOME CONNECTION Have your child name each picture. Then ask your child to explain his or her choice of words to trace.

Extra Support
Catch a Dream • Lesson 6

▶ **Read about the fish. Circle and write the word that completes each sentence.**

I have a fish. She swims fast. I call her Flash. Flash has fins. They help her swim. She swims in a fish tank. We put rocks and plants in the tank, too. Flash likes the plants.

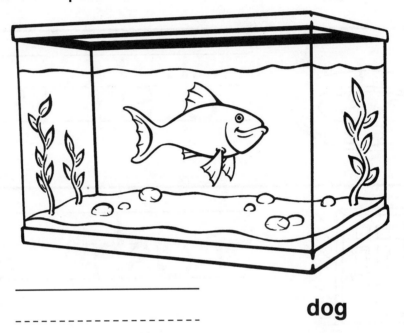

_____

1. Flash is a _____.

dog

fish

_____

2. _____ help Flash swim.

Fins

Plants

_____

3. Flash likes the _____.

rocks

plants

SCHOOL-HOME CONNECTION Have your child read you the sentences he or she completed about the fish. Then ask your child for other details about the fish.

▶ **Trace the word that names each picture.**

1.  truck   trip

2.  flag   frog

3. 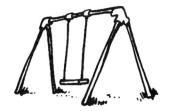 snap   swing

4.  dress   drum

5.  sled   skunk

6.  stop   swim

 SCHOOL-HOME CONNECTION Ask your child
to read all the words on the page and then tell
you why she or he traced certain words.

 47

Extra Support
Catch a Dream • Lesson 6

Level Three

Here and There

Name _____

▶ **Say each picture name. If it has the /ch/ sound you hear in the word <u>chin</u>, trace <u>ch</u>. If the name does not have the /ch/ sound, cross out the letters.**

1.

ch

2.

ch

3.

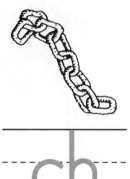

ch

4.

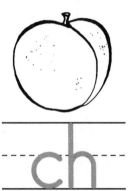

ch

5.

ch

6.

ch

7.

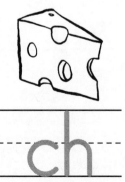

ch

8.

ch

9.

ch

SCHOOL-HOME CONNECTION Have your child say the picture names that have the /ch/ sound. Then have your child practice writing the letters *ch*.

3

Extra Support
Here and There • Lesson 1

Name _____

▶ **Look at each picture. Read the words in the row. Circle the word that names the picture.**

1.

chin   spin

2.

kick   chick

3.

past   patch

4.

catch   cats

5.

pill   pitch

SCHOOL-HOME CONNECTION Ask your child to read aloud the words he or she circled. Then have your child practice writing words containing *ch*.

5

Extra Support
Here and There • Lesson 1

Name _____

▶ **Look at each picture and read the sentence. Circle the word that completes each sentence. Then write the word.**

live   leg

_____

- - - - - - - - - - - - - - -

1. Many animals _____ around here.

Ants   Soon

_____

- - - - - - - - - - - - - - -

2. _____ we will see the bats.

---

taps   turns

_____

- - - - - - - - - - - - - - -

3. When day _____ into night, the bats come out.

---

fly   last

_____

- - - - - - - - - - - - - - -

4. They _____ in the air.

TRY THIS Draw a picture of an animal that can fly.

 SCHOOL-HOME CONNECTION Read the sentences with your child. Ask your child to tell what is happening in each picture.

6

Extra Support
Here and There • Lesson 1

Name _____

▶ **Look at each picture. Trace the word that completes the sentence. Then read the sentence.**

1. He will ___pitch___ the ball.

2. "That is ___such___ a good hit!"

3. She will ___dash___ away.

4. Now the dog will ___fetch___ it.

© Harcourt

SCHOOL-HOME CONNECTION Ask your child to read the first sentence aloud to you. Then ask your child to find two words that end with *tch*.

7

Extra Support
Here and There • Lesson 1

Name _____

▶ **Name each picture. Trace the letters that stand for the beginning sounds.**

1.

cl   fl

2.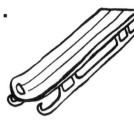

sl   fl

3.

cl   sl

4.

cl   pl

5.

cl   sl

6.

sl   fl

7.

pl   cl

8.

cl   fl

9.

sl   cl

SCHOOL-HOME CONNECTION Ask your child to name the pictures on this page. Talk about the beginning sounds in each word.

8

Extra Support
Here and There • Lesson 1

© Harcourt

▶ **Say the name of the first picture in each row. Circle the picture whose name rhymes with the first picture name.**

1.      

2.          

3.         

4.          

5.      

SCHOOL-HOME CONNECTION Ask your child to name the first picture in each row. Then have your child practice writing words that have *ar*.

10

Extra Support
Here and There • Lesson 2

Name _____

▶ **Look at each picture. Read the two words. Circle and trace the word that names the picture.**

1.

   cat
   car

   car

2.

   barn
   bin

   barn

3.

   jar
   jam

   jar

4.

   stem
   star

   star

5.

   bat
   bar

   bar

 **SCHOOL-HOME CONNECTION** Have your child read aloud the words he or she traced on this page. Then ask your child to practice writing the words *car* and *barn*.

12

Extra Support
Here and There • Lesson 2

© Harcourt

Name _____

▶ **Look at each picture and read the sentence. Circle the word that completes the sentence.**

house   lock

1. Mr. Small lives in a little _____.

shell   city

2. It is in a big _____.

raft   there

3. Sometimes I go to see him _____.

take   tall

4. I _____ my dog with me.

TRY THIS   Draw a picture of a little house. Write the word *house.*

SCHOOL-HOME CONNECTION Ask your child to tell you what is happening in the pictures on this page. Together, read the sentences.

13

Extra Support
Here and There • Lesson 2

Name _____

▶ **Look at each picture. Trace the word that completes the sentence.**

1. Is this your ___car___ ?

2. Yes, but it will not ___start___ .

3. This is too ___hard___ !

4. We can walk to the ___farm___ .

5. It is not ___far___ .

SCHOOL-HOME CONNECTION Ask your child to read aloud one of the sentences he or she completed. Then talk about the sound that the letters *ar* stand for in the word.

14

Extra Support
Here and There • Lesson 2

© Harcourt

▶ **Look at each story picture. Then look at the little pictures. Circle the little picture that shows where the story takes place.**

1.

2.

 SCHOOL-HOME CONNECTION Ask your child to tell you about the two story scenes shown here. Let your child describe what might happen in each story.

15

Extra Support
Here and There • Lesson 2

▶ **Look at each each picture. Trace the word that completes each sentence.**

jump + ed

1. Two little dogs _jumped_ .

jump + s

2. One more dog _jumps_ .

jump + ing

3. Now the big dogs are _jumping_ .

walk + ing

4. The little dogs are _walking_ away.

walk + s

5. One dog _walks_ back.

 SCHOOL-HOME CONNECTION Ask your child to read aloud the second sentence on this page. Then talk about the word endings that were added to the base words.

16

© Harcourt

▶ **Say each picture name. Trace <u>qu</u> if the name begins like the word <u>quick</u>. Trace <u>wh</u> if the name begins like the word <u>what</u>. Cross out the other letter pair.**

1. qu wh

2. qu wh

3. qu wh

4. qu wh

5. qu wh

6. qu wh

7. qu wh

8. qu wh

SCHOOL-HOME CONNECTION Have your child name the first four pictures on this page. Then help your child practice writing the letter pairs *qu* and *wh*.

Extra Support
Here and There • Lesson 3

Name _____

▶ **Look at each picture. Read the words in that row. Trace the picture name. Cross out the other word.**

1.  quilt   tilt

2.  stack   quack

3.  quiz   spill

4.  hen   when

5. 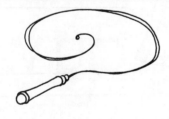 whip   trip

 **SCHOOL-HOME CONNECTION** Ask your child to read aloud the words he or she traced. Then help your child practice reading the words on the page.

20

Extra Support
Here and There • Lesson 3

Name _____

► **Look at each picture and read the sentence. Circle the word that completes the sentence.**

fish   family

1. My _____ likes books about plants.

read   run

2. We _____ books by Mr. Grow as we work.

gum   grew

3. See how big our plants _____.

digging   writing

4. We are _____ a book about our plants.

TRY THIS   Draw a picture about a book you like.

SCHOOL-HOME CONNECTION Ask your child to tell you about the pictures and to read aloud the sentences.

21

Extra Support
Here and There • Lesson 3

Name _____

▶ **Look at each picture. Trace the word that completes the sentence.**

1. _____When_____ can we stop?

2. Don't _____quit_____ now.

3. _____Which_____ path is right?

4. Let's try _____this_____ one.

5. Be as _____quick_____ as you can!

 **SCHOOL-HOME CONNECTION** Ask your child to read aloud the sentences she or he completed. Then talk about the letters that stand for the beginning sounds in the words your child traced. (wh, qu, th)   **22**

Extra Support
Here and There • Lesson 3

Name _____

▶ **The pictures in the box tell a story. Think about the characters in the story.**

▶ **Circle the picture of the main character. Make a check ✔on the pictures of two other story characters.**

SCHOOL-HOME CONNECTION Have your child tell you the story shown in the pictures. Talk about the characters.

23

Extra Support
Here and There • Lesson 3

Name _____

► **Look at each picture. Read the words in the row. Trace the picture name. Cross out the other word.**

1. 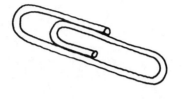 clip lip

2.  rag flag

3.  plug rug

4.  shed sled

5.  sock clock

SCHOOL-HOME CONNECTION Have your child name the pictures on this page. Talk about the letters that stand for the beginning sounds of the words. (*cl, fl, pl, sl*)

24

Extra Support
Here and There • Lesson 3

▶ **Look at each picture. Read the words in the row. Trace the picture name. Cross out the other word.**

1.  grid girl

2.  fern farm

3.  bring bird

4.  tan turn

5.  curb cub

SCHOOL-HOME CONNECTION Ask your child to read aloud the words he or she traced on this page. Then have your child practice writing the word *girl*.

26

Extra Support
Here and There • Lesson 4

Name _____

▶ **Look at each picture. Read the question.**
Circle <u>yes</u> or <u>no</u> to answer the question.

1. Can it turn?   **yes**   **no**

2. Can it purr?   **yes**   **no**

3. Can it have fur?   **yes**   **no**

4. Is she the first?   **yes**   **no**

5. Can it live in the dirt?   **yes**   **no**

SCHOOL-HOME CONNECTION Have your
child read aloud a question. Ask how your
child figured out how to answer the question.

28

Extra Support
Here and There • Lesson 4

Name _____

▶ **Look at each picture and read the sentence. Circle the word that completes the sentence.**

way   web

1. Have you found the _____ to the four big swings?

card   were

2. There _____ four small swings back there.

full   for

3. The park is _____ of these little swings.

fur   find

4. If you _____ the big swings, we will follow you.

TRY THIS What would you like to find? Draw a picture of it.

SCHOOL-HOME CONNECTION Ask your child to tell you about what is happening on this page. Together, read the sentences your child completed.

29

Extra Support
Here and There • Lesson 4

Name _____

► **Look at each picture. Trace the word that completes the sentence.**

1. Look at the __birds__!

2. Is the first one a __duck__?

3. The __third__ one is not a duck.

4. Have you __met__ that girl?

5. The third bird is __her__ pet.

SCHOOL-HOME CONNECTION Ask your child to read aloud some of the sentences on the page. Have your child read the words she or he traced.

30

Extra Support
Here and There • Lesson 4

© Harcourt

► **Look at the big picture. Think of a story that goes with the picture. Circle the little picture that shows where the story takes place.**

1.

2.

SCHOOL-HOME CONNECTION Ask your child to describe the two story settings he or she circled. Together, make up a story that could take place in one of the settings.

Extra Support
Here and There • Lesson 4

Name _____

▶ **Look at each picture. Trace the word that completes the sentence.**

1. call + ed

Liz __called__ last night.

2. call + ing

She is __calling__ back.

3. ring + s

It __rings__.

4. ring + ing

It is still __ringing__.

5. pick + s

Jeff __picks__ it up.

SCHOOL-HOME CONNECTION Ask your child to read aloud the sentences on the page. Talk about what the endings -ed and -ing mean when they are at the end of a verb.

32

Extra Support
Here and There • Lesson 4

© Harcourt

▶ Say each picture name. If it has the same
ending sound as the word <u>little</u>, trace <u>le</u>. If the name
does not end with that sound, cross out the letters.

1.

le

2.

le

3.

le

4.

le

5.

le

6.

le

7.

le

8.

le

9.

le

SCHOOL-HOME CONNECTION Ask your child
which picture names end with the same sound
you hear at the end of *little*. With your child,
think of more words that have the same ending.

Extra Support
Here and There • Lesson 5

© Harcourt

▶ **Look at each picture. Read the words in the row. Trace the picture name. Cross out the other word.**

1.  lantern   little

2.  plaster   pickle

3.  turtle   turnip

4. apple   antler

5. catfish   candle

 TRY THIS Draw a picture of something that has the same ending sound as the word <u>little</u>.

 SCHOOL-HOME CONNECTION Ask your child to read aloud the words he or she traced. Talk about what is the same and what is different about the words.

36

© Harcourt

Name _____

▶ **Look at each picture and read the sentence. Trace the word that completes the sentence. Cross out the word that does not belong.**

1. Our school saddle
is a great place!

2. All my friends get today
together here.

3. We talk ten and play.

4. We help each egg
other, too.

 Draw a picture of you and a friend together.

 SCHOOL-HOME CONNECTION Have your
child read aloud the sentences on the page.
Then ask your child why he or she traced
those words.

37

Extra Support
Here and There • Lesson 5

Name _____

▶ **Look at each picture. Trace the word that completes the sentence. Cross out the word that does not belong.**

1. Oh, no! Don't  truck

   tickle me!

2. You will make me glitter

   giggle!

3. Then I'll fall into the puddle

   porch.

SCHOOL-HOME CONNECTION Ask your child to read aloud one of the sentences on this page. Then help your child practice writing the word she or he traced.

38

Extra Support
Here and There • Lesson 5

© Harcourt

Name _____

▶ **Look at the picture. Trace the word that completes each sentence.**

Skip   Tip   Pip

1. Skip is ___small___.

2. Tip is ___smaller___ than Skip.

3. Pip is the ___smallest___ of all.

4. Pip is the ___fastest___ one, too.

SCHOOL-HOME CONNECTION Have your
child read aloud the first two sentences on the
page. Talk about the word endings -er and -est
and what they mean.

39

Extra Support
Here and There • Lesson 5

Name _____

▶ **Say both picture names. Circle and color the picture whose name has the same vowel sound as the word <u>toad</u>.**

1.

2.

3.

4.

5.

6.

7.

8.

Extra Support
Here and There • Lesson 6

© Harcourt

▶ **Look at the picture. Read the words in the row. Trace the picture name. Cross out the other words.**

1.  bud bow

2.  toad tick

3. got goat

4. bell bowl

5. coat cot

SCHOOL-HOME CONNECTION Have your child read aloud the words he or she traced. Talk about the letters that stand for the long *o* sound in the words.

43

Name _____

▶ **Look at each picture and read the sentence. Trace the word that completes the sentence. Cross out the word that does not belong.**

1. Who Would is
at the door?

2. Live Would
you go and see?

3. I made kind
these for you.

4. How kind made
you are!

TRY THIS Draw a picture of something you made. Write about your picture. Use the word <u>made</u>.

SCHOOL-HOME CONNECTION Have your child read aloud the sentences on this page. Talk about the meanings of the words she or he traced.

44

Extra Support
Here and There • Lesson 6

Name _____

▶ **Look at each picture. Trace the word that completes the sentence.**

1. Here comes the

big _goat_!

2. He's jumping into our

boat.

3. Will it still _float_?

4. We can use this _mop_.

5. I am glad it's a _hot_ day!

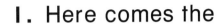
SCHOOL-HOME CONNECTION Ask your child to read one or two sentences on this page. Talk about the different sounds *o* stands for in the words your child traced.

45

Extra Support
Here and There • Lesson 6

▶ **Look at the big picture. Think of a story that goes with the picture. Circle the small picture that shows a character who could be in the same story.**

1.

2.

SCHOOL-HOME CONNECTION Have your child describe the two large pictures on this page. Ask how your child decided which character could be part of each story.

46

Extra Support
Here and There • Lesson 6

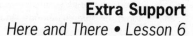

Name _____

▶ **Look at each picture. Trace the word that completes the sentence.**

like + s

1. Bill's dad _likes_ boats.

row + ed

2. He _rowed_ a little boat.

row + ing

3. Now he is _rowing_ a big boat.

row + s

4. He _rows_ around the pond.

swim + s

5. Bill's mom _swims_ to the boat.

SCHOOL-HOME CONNECTION Ask your child to read the sentences. Then take turns saying sentences that include words with the endings: -s, -ed, -ing.

Extra Support
Here and There • Lesson 6

Level Four

Time Together

Name _____

▶ **Trace the word that names the picture.
Cross out the other word.**

1. send she

2. bee bat

3. sleep slip

4. eat at

5. lip leap

6. patch peach

 SCHOOL-HOME CONNECTION Have your
child tell why he or she traced each word.
Then have your child practice writing words
that have the letter *e*.

9

► **Circle the words that have the same vowel sound as the word <u>bee</u>. Then do what the sentence tells you.**

1. Ann strings beads.

Color the beads red.

2. Don has some beets.

Color the beets purple.

3. This bird has a big beak.

Color the bird's beak.

4. The seal has a ball.

Color the seal.

 SCHOOL-HOME CONNECTION Ask your child to point to all of the words that have the long *e* sound, as in *bee*. Then have your child write five more words that have the long *e* sound.

11

Extra Support
Time Together • Lesson 1

Name _____

▶ **Look at each picture and read the sentence. Trace the word that completes the sentence.**

1. Do you ___know___ anything about cats?

2. Should the kitten be ___moved___?

3. I have ___room___ for only one.

4. I will ___write___ an ad for those.

SCHOOL-HOME CONNECTION Read the sentences with your child. Talk about the words your child traced. Encourage her or him to say sentences that use the words.

12

Extra Support
Time Together • Lesson 1

Name _____

▶ **Trace the word that names the picture.
Cross out the other word.**

1. Dean   Jean

2. boat   bees

3. jeans   Joan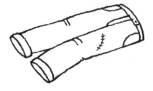

4. peel   bowl

5. coat   seat

6. road   read

SCHOOL-HOME CONNECTION Ask your child
to read aloud the words he or she has traced.
Then have your child make up a sentence for
each word.

13

Extra Support
Time Together • Lesson 1

Name _____

▶ **The letters in each group are in ABC, or alphabetical, order. Say the letters to yourself as you trace them.**

1. h i j k

2. p q r s

3. b d f g

4. r t v x

5. l n o q

SCHOOL-HOME CONNECTION Sing the alphabet song with your child. Then have your child read aloud the letters in each group. Ask your child how he or she knows the letters are in alphabetical order.

14

Extra Support
Time Together • Lesson 1

▶ **Read each pair of sentences. Complete the second sentence by tracing the contraction that means the same as the underlined words.**

1. <u>She is</u> looking at cats.

She's going

to get a new cat.

2. She <u>does not</u> want a dog.

She _doesn't_ have room for a dog.

3. <u>She will</u> take the black and white kitten.

She'll brush it every day.

4. <u>He is</u> going to miss the kitten.

_He's_ sad to see the kitten go.

SCHOOL-HOME CONNECTION With your child, make a list of words that make contractions with 's, n't, and 'll.

15

Extra Support
Time Together • Lesson 1

▶ **Trace the word that completes each sentence. Cross out the other word.**

1. Jane went to the _<u>lake</u>_ _<u>last</u>_ .

2. She ate some _<u>grass</u>_ _<u>grapes</u>_ .

3. She wanted to _<u>save</u>_ _<u>shack</u>_ some for her friend.

4. Soon _<u>Jane's</u>_ _<u>Jim's</u>_ friend came to see her.

5. They had a _<u>rack</u>_ _<u>race</u>_ around the lake.

 SCHOOL-HOME CONNECTION Talk with your child about how he or she chose the words to trace. Then have your child think of two rhyming words for these words: *lake, page,* and *race*.

17

▶ **Trace the word. Draw a line to the picture that matches it.**

1.

2.

3.

4. gate

5.

SCHOOL-HOME CONNECTION Help your child make a list of five words that have the *a-e* pattern.

19

Extra Support
Time Together • Lesson 2

Name _____

▶ **Look at each picture and read the sentence. Trace the word that completes the sentence.**

1. Our ___country___ is

the United States of America.

2. ___Earth___ is the third

planet from the sun.

3. Sam wants to go all over the

___world___.

4. They go to a special place, far from

___town___, for picnics.

SCHOOL-HOME CONNECTION Ask your child to make up his or her own sentences using the words *country, Earth, over, special, town,* and *world.*

20

Extra Support
Time Together • Lesson 2

▶ **Trace the word that has the same vowel sound as in <u>gate</u>. Circle the word that has the same vowel sound as in <u>cat</u>.**

1.

2. pan

pane

3. mate mat

4. can cane

5. tape tap

SCHOOL-HOME CONNECTION Have your child practice writing these pairs of words: *rate-rat, cane-can,* and *tape-tap.*

Name _____

▶ **Read the words in the box. Write the words where they belong on the chart.**

house	pond	plane	truck
hill	car	bus	cave

Things That Move	Things That Do Not Move
truck	house

SCHOOL-HOME CONNECTION Have your child read aloud the words he or she wrote in both lists. Together, name two more things that move and two more things that do not move.

22

Extra Support
Time Together • Lesson 2

Name _____

▶ **Trace the words in the chart.**

	ed	ing
name	named	naming
race	raced	racing
fade	faded	fading

▶ **Write the word that completes each sentence.**

_____

1. They _____ the shop "Sam's Place."

_____

2. They are _____
to the shop.

▶ **Draw a line from the picture to the word that names it. Then trace the word.**

1.

cherry

2.

happy

3.

penny

4.

sixty

5.

soapy

6.

sandy

SCHOOL-HOME CONNECTION Write the following words in a list: *fish, jump, boss, chill,* and *fluff.* Have your child write the letter *y* after each one and then read the new words to you.

25

Name _____

▶ **Trace the word that best completes each sentence. Cross out the other word.**

1. Sally has a _____ .

bunny box

2. Betty has a baby _____ .

buggy bug

3. Sally's pet is _____ .

happy heat

4. The wheel gets _____ .

digging dirty

5. The street is _____ .

harm hilly

SCHOOL-HOME CONNECTION Write the following words in a list: *leaf, sleep, arm, grass,* and *trick*. Have your child write the letter *y* after each one and then read the new words to you.

Extra Support
Time Together • Lesson 3

Name _____

▶ **Look at each picture and read each sentence. Trace the word that completes the sentence.**

1. One big stick can ___hold___ up the tent above them.

2. People live in

___different___ places.

3. The ___water___ is warm.

4. The garden is many ___years___ old.

 SCHOOL-HOME CONNECTION Read the sentences with your child. Talk about how the sentences match the pictures.

28

Extra Support
Time Together • Lesson 3

Name _____

► Trace the word that completes each
   sentence. Cross out the other word.

1. Carly is having a

   party pansy .

2. The cake has a

   cheese cherry

   topping.

3. The children hurry handle

   to run the race.

4. Carly got gifts with

   thin thirty ribbons.

5. They all had a

   very later good time.

SCHOOL-HOME CONNECTION Have your
child read each sentence. Then ask how the
picture matches the sentence.

29

Extra Support
Time Together • Lesson 3

Name _____

▶ **Read all three lists. Circle the two lists with things that match the title. Then trace the words in those two lists.**

Animals in the Air

bird

bee

plane

Animals in the Water

sunfish

starfish

whale

Animals on the Land

cat

goat

sheep

Extra Support
Time Together • Lesson 3

© Harcourt

Name _____

▶ **Trace the word that completes each sentence. Cross out the other word.**

1. The girls 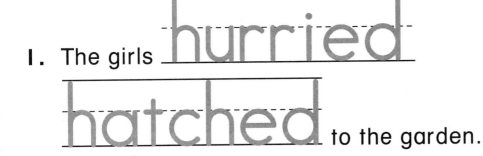 hurried

    hatched to the garden.

2. The bird  films flies above them.

3. The dog helps hurries

    away with the bone.

4. The girls eat berries

    beetles for dessert.

5. She treated tried to

    clean up.

 **SCHOOL-HOME CONNECTION** Discuss with your child how the pictures match the sentences. Ask your child to explain his or her answer choices. **31**

Extra Support
Time Together • Lesson 3

▶ Trace the words that have the same vowel sound as the word <u>mine</u>. Cross out the other word.

1. time tame

2. van vine

3. rise rose

4. bake bike

5. pine pin

 SCHOOL-HOME CONNECTION Have your child say each pair of words and explain why he or she chose each answer. Then help your child list two rhyming words for each of these words: *time, vine,* and *bike.*

 33

© Harcourt

Name _____

▶ **Trace the word that answers the question or completes the sentence. Cross out the other word.**

1. Where do bees live?

   hive   time

2. You _____ your friends.

   rice   like

3. A _____ on a bus can be fun.

   ride   nine

4. Who has a wedding?

   side   bride

5. What is the color of snow?

   white   nice

 SCHOOL-HOME CONNECTION Ask your child to say the words that have the same vowel sound as in *mine*. Help your child think of rhyming words for each correct answer.

(35)

Extra Support
Time Together • Lesson 4

© Harcourt

Name _____

▶ **Look at each picture and read the sentence. Trace the word that completes the sentence.**

1. They _____ cook _____ because it is dinner time.

2. They _____ listen _____ for Pat at the front door.

3. Most people can

_____ picture _____ food they like.

4. Do you know why

_____ young _____ people like sweets?

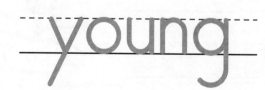

SCHOOL-HOME CONNECTION Read the sentences with your child. Talk about how the sentences describe what is happening in the pictures.

36

Extra Support
Time Together • Lesson 4

© Harcourt

Name _____

▶ **Trace the word that names the picture.**
Cross out the other word.

1. bite   bib

2. fine   fin

3. dim   dime

4. kit   kite

5. fit   file

SCHOOL-HOME CONNECTION Ask your child to point to all of the words that have the long *i* sound, as in *five*. Then have your child point to all of the words that have the short *i* sound, as in *sit*.

37

Extra Support
Time Together • Lesson 4

Name _____

▶ **Read the words in each set. Circle the group that has all its words in ABC order. Then trace the words in that group.**

★

1.

ball   call   doll

♥

doll   call   ball

★

2.

sag   rag   tag

♥

rag   sag   tag

★

3.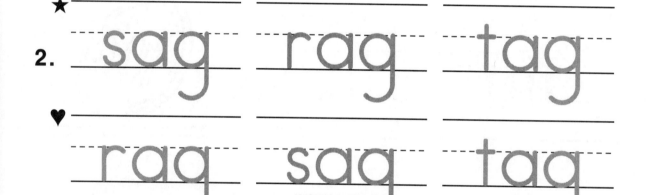

lap   nap   map

♥

lap   map   nap

SCHOOL-HOME CONNECTION Have your child read aloud the words in each group he or she circled. Then sing the alphabet song together.

38

Extra Support
Time Together • Lesson 4

► **Trace the contraction that means the same as the underlined words. Cross out the other contraction.**

1. She is  reading.

2. She <u>did not</u> doesn't didn't finish the story.

3. <u>They will</u> They'll You'll eat dinner.

4. <u>She will</u> She's She'll finish the story.

 SCHOOL-HOME CONNECTION Have your child read each sentence and explain his or her answer choice. Then have your child practice writing words with the contractions 's, n't, and 'll.

39

Extra Support
Time Together • Lesson 4

Name _____

► Trace the word that names the picture.
Cross out the other word.

1. country   city

2. cent   since

3. pencil   patch

4. prince   purse

5. dock   dance

6. stack   space

 SCHOOL-HOME CONNECTION Have your child
tell why he or she traced each word. Then have
your child practice writing the letter *c* in some
of the words on the page.

 41

Name _____

▶ **Trace the word that best matches the clue. Cross out the other word.**

1. You try to run faster than the other people.

face   race

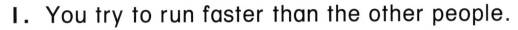

2. You smile with this.

face   race

3. A good and kind person is this.

ice   nice

4. You hear a song and move to the beat.

dance   glance

5. This means "2 times."

rice   twice

SCHOOL-HOME CONNECTION Help your child name one more rhyming word for each pair of answer choices (examples: *trace, brace, mice, prance,* and *price*). Then ask your child to write one of the new rhyming words.

43

Extra Support
Time Together • Lesson 5

Name _____

▶ **Look at each picture and read the sentence. Trace the word that completes the sentence.**

1. Spencer almost _always_ wins the race.

2. He does not _even_ seem to try.

3. Once, he won a _pretty_ ribbon.

4. They say the _sound_ of cheers is the best.

SCHOOL-HOME CONNECTION Read the sentences with your child. Talk about the words your child traced.

44

Extra Support
Time Together • Lesson 5

Name _____

▶ **Trace the word that names the picture.**
Cross out the other word.

1. lace   space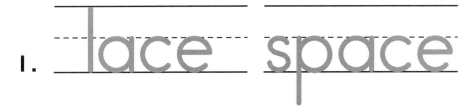

2. mice   rice

3. space   trace

4. price   ice

5. trace   space

SCHOOL-HOME CONNECTION Ask your child to read aloud the words he or she has traced. Then have your child practice writing the letters *ace* and *ice*.

45

Extra Support
Time Together • Lesson 5

▶ **Trace the word that best completes the sentence. Cross out the other word.**

I. She likes to

<u>rice ride</u>.

2. The <u>price pride</u>

is low.

3. The <u>mice bride</u>

wore white.

4. Do you like <u>rice tide</u>?

5. It is low <u>twice tide</u>.

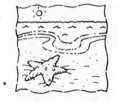

 SCHOOL-HOME CONNECTION Ask your child to explain his or her answer choices. Then have your child practice writing the letters *ice* and *ide* in words. **46**

Extra Support
Time Together • Lesson 5

Name _____

▶ **Circle and color the picture in each row whose name rhymes with the first picture in the row.**

1.

clown

2.

cow

3.

loud

4.

sour

5.

shower

SCHOOL-HOME CONNECTION With your child, make a list of five words that have the vowel sound /ou/, as in *crown* and *loud*.

48

Extra Support
Time Together • Lesson 6

Name _____

▶ **Trace the word that completes each sentence. Cross out the other word.**

1. We need a _pound loud_ of flour.

2. Howard went into _crowd town_.

3. He got some _ground out_ beef.

4. He _round found_ a dollar.

5. He got some _flowers powders_.

SCHOOL-HOME CONNECTION Talk with your child about the two ways the vowel sound is spelled in the words he or she traced and crossed out.

50

Extra Support
Time Together • Lesson 6

Name _____

► **Look at each picture and read the sentence. Trace the word that completes the sentence.**

1. Kevin takes care of ___eight___ pets.

2. Kevin took his dog to see ___Dr.___ Brown.

3. The vet was very ___busy___.

4. Does she have ___any___ time for Fred?

SCHOOL-HOME CONNECTION Ask your child to make up his or her own sentences using the words *any, busy, care, Dr., eight,* and *took.*

51

Extra Support
Time Together • Lesson 6

Name _____

▶ **Trace the word that names the picture.**
Cross out the other word.

1.  clown couch

2.  ounce pouch

3.  towel town

4.  cloud scout

5.  power how

SCHOOL-HOME CONNECTION Ask your child to say each picture name and think of a word that rhymes with it.

52

Name _____

▶ **Read all four lists. Circle the lists with things in them that match the title. Then trace the words in those lists.**

Words About Time

now

black

soon

Words About Color

red

green

pink

Words About Feelings

sad

glad

proud

Words About Places

house

clock

city

SCHOOL-HOME CONNECTION Have your child read aloud the words in the lists he or she circled. Then ask what other words could be added to those lists.

53

Extra Support
Time Together • Lesson 6

Name _____

▶ **Trace the word that goes with the picture. Cross out the other word.**

1.  frown   town

2.  gown   down

3.  pound   round

4.  sound   ground

5. clown   brown

SCHOOL-HOME CONNECTION Ask your child to explain his or her answer choices. Then have your child practice writing words with *own* and *ound*.

Extra Support
Time Together • Lesson 6

► **Draw a line from each picture to the
word that names it. Then trace the word.**

1.

_____
pie

2.

_____
fries

3.

_____
tie

4.

_____
sky

5.

_____
fly

6.

_____
cry

SCHOOL-HOME CONNECTION Have your
child practice writing words that end with the
letter *y* or the letters *ie*.

56

Extra Support
Time Together • Lesson 7

▶ **Trace the word that best completes each sentence. Cross out the other word.**

1. This is ___my by___ bear.

2. He needs a new ___fry tie___.

3. Do you know ___cry why___ he needs it?

4. Some friends are coming ___by fry___.

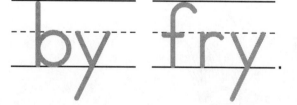

5. We will have some tea and ___sky pie___.

SCHOOL-HOME CONNECTION Have your
child practice writing the crossed-out words.

58

Extra Support
Time Together • Lesson 7

▶ **Read each sentence. Write the word from the box that completes the sentence.**

love	Hello	high	opened

_____

1. Ty _____ the door.

_____

2. "_____, Sly. I'm

glad to see you again," said Ty.

_____

3. "Let's fly kites up _____

in the blue sky," said Sly.

_____

4. "I would _____ to,"

said Ty.

Name _____

▶ **Trace the word that completes the sentence. Cross out the other word.**

1. Becky wanted to _____ tie ___ cry _____ a bow.

2. She _____ fried ___ tried _____ three times.

3. "Tying a bow is _____ tricky ___ dusty _____," said Becky's mom.

4. "Do not _____ sleepy ___ worry _____. I will help you," she said.

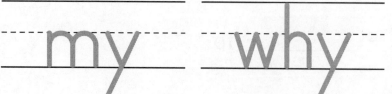

5. "Thank you," said Becky. "Now

_____ my ___ why _____ gift looks nice."

SCHOOL-HOME CONNECTION Have your child read each sentence. Then ask him or her to explain how she or he knew which words to trace and cross out.

60

Extra Support
Time Together • Lesson 7

▶ **Read the names in each pair of groups.**
Circle the group with all the names in ABC order.
Then trace the names in that group.

★
1. Jan   Kim   Liz   Max

♥ Ann   Cal   Bill   Dot

★
2. Art   Brad   Dan   Carl

♥ Ed   Fran   Gil   Hal

★
3. Ken   Mel   Ron   Nat

♥ Pat   Sam   Tim   Will

SCHOOL-HOME CONNECTION Have your
child read aloud the names in each group he
or she circled. Then ask your child to put the
names from one of the other groups into
alphabetical order.

61

Extra Support
Time Together • Lesson 7

Name _____

▶ **Trace the word that completes each sentence. Cross out the other word.**

1. He's He'll

my friend.

2. He wasn't doesn't

have a dog, but I do.

3. She'll Haven't

run after the ball.

4. Didn't She's

a very good dog.

SCHOOL-HOME CONNECTION Discuss with your child how the pictures show what the sentences mean. Ask your child to explain her or his answer choices.

62

Extra Support
Time Together • Lesson 7

Name _____

▶ **Trace the word that has the vowel sound in home. Cross out the other word.**

1. bone ban

2. rob robe

3. rose rise

4. pill pole

5. home ham

SCHOOL-HOME CONNECTION Have your child say each pair of words and explain why he or she chose each answer.

64

Extra Support
Time Together • Lesson 8

Name _____

▶ **Trace the word that answers the question or completes the sentence. Cross out the other word.**

1. Where does a king sit?

throne grove

2. If you said something, you ____.

spoke drove

3. She ____ you like the cake.

zones hopes

4. It's part of your face.

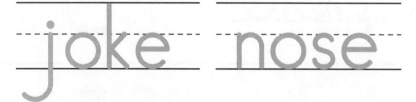
joke nose

5. You do this to a door.

close rope

SCHOOL-HOME CONNECTION Ask your child to read the words that have the same vowel sound as *home*. Help your child think of rhyming words for each correct answer.

66

Extra Support
Time Together • Lesson 8

Name _____

▶ **Look at each picture and read the sentence. Trace the word that completes the sentence.**

1. The bee went from one ___field___ to another.

2. There she found

___twelve___ wild flowers.

3. The flowers wait for a bee to

___touch___ them.

4. A bee can ___change___ nectar into honey.

SCHOOL-HOME CONNECTION Read the sentences with your child. Talk about the words your child traced. Together, think of new sentences that use the words.

67

Name _____

▶ **Trace the word that tells about the picture. Cross out the other word.**

1.
joke   job

2.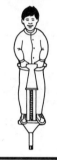
hope   hop

3.
bone   bond

4.
rode   rod

5.
pose   pot

SCHOOL-HOME CONNECTION Ask your child to point to the words that have the long *o* sound, as in *home.* Then have your child point to the words with the short *o* sound, as in *dot.* Finally, have your child practice writing the letter *o.*

68

Name _____

▶ **Trace the word that completes the sentence. Cross out the other word.**

1. The bee is

black blast

and yellow.

2. The bees

flag fly

out of the hive.

3. The bees find some

flames

flowers.

4. A flock float

of sheep is here.

 SCHOOL-HOME CONNECTION Have your child read each sentence and explain his or her answer choice. Then have your child practice writing words that begin with *bl* and *fl*.

 69

Extra Support
Time Together • Lesson 8

· TROPHIES ·

Level Five

Gather Around

Name _____

▶ **Trace the word that goes with the picture. Cross out the other word.**

1. right night

2. light sigh

3. high sight

4. bright might

5. fright tight

SCHOOL-HOME CONNECTION With your child, make a list of words that rhyme with *right* and have the same *-ight* spelling.

③

Extra Support
Gather Around • Lesson 1

Name _____

▶ **Trace the word that answers the question or completes the sentence. Cross out the other word.**

1. The top of a hill is _____.

high right

2. When do you go to bed?

sight night

3. The sun is _____.

bright tight

4. If it's dark, turn on the _____.

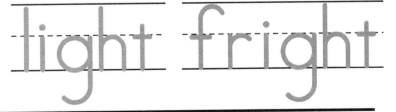
light fright

5. The sad boy gave a big _____.

sigh might

SCHOOL-HOME CONNECTION Discuss with your child how the vowel sound is spelled in the words on the lines.

Extra Support
Gather Around • Lesson 1

Name _____

▶ **Look at each picture and read the sentence. Trace the word that completes the sentence.**

1. I _thought_ birds liked

to fly.

2. I wonder if he's _afraid_.

3. His mom will help him

.

4. _Nothing_ can stop him now!

5. He flew off to _join_ his friends.

SCHOOL-HOME CONNECTION Help your child write two more sentences to continue the story. Have your child use one of the traced words in the sentences.

6

Extra Support
Gather Around • Lesson 1

Name _____

 *Phonics*
CVVC and
***-igh* Words**

▶ Trace the word that goes with the picture. Cross out the other word.

1. boat   coat

2. tight   fight

3. high   bright

4. beach   meat

5. night   sigh

 SCHOOL-HOME CONNECTION Read all the words with your child. Help her or him think of and write a word that rhymes with each of the traced words.

▲ **7**

Extra Support
Gather Around • Lesson 1

Name _____

▶ **Read the story. Then follow the directions.**

The wind and the sun were talking about who was stronger. They saw a man walking. The wind said, "I can make that man take off his coat." The wind huffed and puffed, but that made the man button his coat. The wind gave up.

Then the sun said, "Watch this." The sun went higher and higher in the sky. The higher the sun went, the warmer it got. At last the man became so hot that he took off his coat.

"See?" said the sun to the wind. "I'm stronger than you."

▶ **Circle the picture that shows something that happened in the story.**

 SCHOOL-HOME CONNECTION Ask your child if he or she was surprised by the story's ending. Then ask your child to point out words in the story with long /i/ spelled -igh.

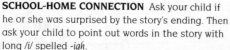

8

Extra Support
Gather Around • Lesson 1

► **Look at each picture and read the sentence. Trace the word that completes the sentence.**

1. The bird ___liked___ to fly high in the sky.

2. He ___raced___ his friend to the birdbath.

3. The birds are ___tasting___ the food.

4. Now a cat is ___chasing___ the birds!

5. The birds ___decided___ to fly off.

SCHOOL-HOME CONNECTION Have your child read each sentence. Then ask her or him to use the words in new sentences.

9

Extra Support
Gather Around • Lesson 1

Name _____

▶ Trace the word that names the picture.
Cross out the other word.

1. pail snail

2. paint pay

3. tray sail

4. train stain
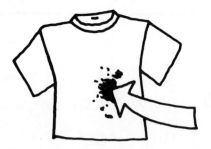

5. ham hay

 11

Extra Support
Gather Around • Lesson 2

Name _____

▶ **Trace the word that completes each sentence. Cross out the other word.**

1. Ray wants to play with his

train nail .

2. Kay can

sail waist her boat.

3. The pup wags its

tail pail .

4. The kids want to

play hay all day.

5. A gray clay

sky can mean rain.

 SCHOOL-HOME CONNECTION Ask your child to explain her or his answers. Then ask what letters stand for the long *a* sound in the traced words.

Extra Support
Gather Around • Lesson 2

Name _____

► **Look at each picture and read the sentence. Trace the word that completes the sentence.**

1. Mr. Jay's son got <u>caught</u> in the rain.

2. He <u>hurried</u> home as fast as he could.

3. At least he was <u>near</u> his house.

4. Now he has a little <u>cold</u>.

5. I'm <u>sure</u> he'll feel better soon.

 SCHOOL-HOME CONNECTION Help your child write a new story containing the traced words.

14

© Harcourt

Name _____

▶ **Trace the word that completes each sentence. Cross out the other word.**

1. Kate likes to

make brake things.

2. Once she made a _____ may clay _____ whale.

3. She painted sailed its

face gray.

4. She baked a big cake hay .

5. She placed the cake on a

flake plate

and gave it to Jake.

SCHOOL-HOME CONNECTION With your child, discuss other presents that can be made rather than bought. Then help your child write more words with the long *a* sound.

 15

Extra Support
Gather Around • Lesson 2

Name _____

▶ **Trace the word that completes each sentence. Cross out the other word.**

1. Blake and Kay are ____.

skating skate

2. Dale is ____ Jan to the gate.

race racing

3. Blake and Kay are ____ each other.

chased chasing

4. Jake ____ at Dad.

waved wave

5. Dad ____ all the fun!

taping taped

SCHOOL-HOME CONNECTION Help your child write sentences using some of the words he or she did not trace.

16

► **Trace the word that completes each sentence. Cross out the other word.**

1. They don't ____ looking for the ball.

find   mind

2. They lost it in the

grind   wild   plants.

3. A   child   mild   will help them look.

4. Did they look

kind   behind   the tree?

5. I think they'll

find   mind   it soon.

 SCHOOL-HOME CONNECTION Help your child make a list of all the words in the activity containing the long i sound spelled i.

18

Extra Support
Gather Around • Lesson 3

▶ **Trace the word that answers the question or completes the sentence. Cross out the other word.**

1. What part of your body do you think with?

2. Someone who is not grown up is a

 .

3. An animal that is not tame is

 .

4. You need to do this to some clocks.

5. She is hiding

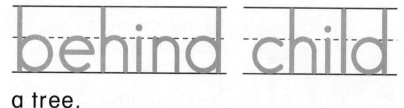 

a tree.

SCHOOL-HOME CONNECTION Help your child make up other riddles and incomplete sentences containing the above answers.

20

Name _____

▶ **Look at each picture and read the sentence. Trace the word that completes the sentence.**

1. We all work hard
 art class.

2. We are almost ready for the big art show.

3. Both Jake and Beth are making a clay animal.

4. At last their animal is ready, too.

 SCHOOL-HOME CONNECTION Talk with your child about favorite art projects she or he has enjoyed. Then have your child practice writing the words he or she traced.

21

Extra Support
Gather Around • Lesson 3

Name _____

▶ **Trace the word that goes with the picture. Cross out the other word.**

1. kite stripe

2. slide find

3. wind wild

4. child hide

5. vine smile

SCHOOL-HOME CONNECTION Help your child make a list of words containing the long i sound spelled *i* or *i-e*.

Extra Support
Gather Around • Lesson 3

© Harcourt

Name _____

▶ **Read the story. Then follow the directions.**

Pets such as cats and dogs have people to feed them. But wild animals must find food for themselves. Bats find bugs. They catch the bugs in the air. Sharks hunt fish. They can hear and smell the fish from far away. Tigers hunt their food, too. Like sharks, they can smell food from far away.

▶ **Now read the sentences. Circle the sentence that tells the most important idea in the story.**

1. Sharks live in the sea.

2. Wild animals have to find food for themselves.

3. Bats catch bugs in the air.

SCHOOL-HOME CONNECTION Read the paragraph with your child. Ask your child to point out words with the long *i* sound.

23

Extra Support
Gather Around • Lesson 3

Name _____

▶ **Trace the word that completes each sentence. Cross out the other word.**

1. Jane is

  the ball.

2. She _____ slam slammed _____ it
good and hard.

3. The pitcher

dropping dropped it.

4. Jane skidding skidded
across the plate.

5. Now all the fans are

clapped clapping.

SCHOOL-HOME CONNECTION Help your child
make a list of verbs ending in *ed* and *ing*. Discuss
whether changes have been made before adding
the ending.

24

Extra Support
Gather Around • Lesson 3

Name _____

▶ **Trace the word that completes each sentence. Cross out the other word.**

1. Most Post

of Jack's friends had pets.

2. Jack told sofa

his mom he wanted a kitten.

3. They went to the animal shelter on a

sold cold day.

4. "May I hold fold

that cat?" Jack asked.

5. " Hello Ago ,

Golden," said Jack to his new pet.

SCHOOL-HOME CONNECTION Help your child make a list of words that contain the long *o* sound, such as *cold, go, post, most, no, bold, old, sold, told, fold, mold, hello, total, folder, soldier.*

26

Extra Support
Gather Around • Lesson 4

Name _____

▶ Trace the word that has the same vowel
  sound as the word <u>go</u>. Cross out the other word.

1. hold held

2. pest post

3. doll old

4. hello hall

5. fast fold

SCHOOL-HOME CONNECTION Help your child
make up sentences containing the words he or she
did not trace. Point out the letter that stands for
the vowel sound in each word.

Extra Support
Gather Around • Lesson 4

Name _____

▶ **Look at each picture and read the sentence. Trace the word that completes the sentence.**

1. A bird ___pulls___ a worm off a tree.

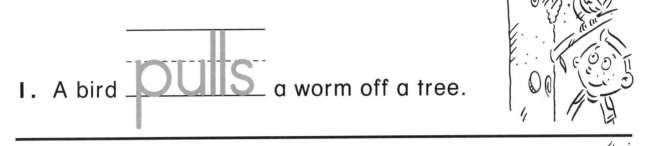

2. Be a ___nature___ detective. Find out why.

3. Look on the forest ___floor___.

4. You might find some ___clues___.

5. Look! There's a ___piece___ of egg shell.

6. Aha! What a good

___detective___!

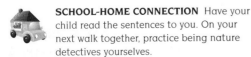 **SCHOOL-HOME CONNECTION** Have your child read the sentences to you. On your next walk together, practice being nature detectives yourselves.

 29

Name _____

▶ **Trace the word that completes the sentence. Cross out the other word.**

1. Most Gold

of the stuff here is old.

2. There's a little

dove hole

in this sofa.

3. One of the dishes is

rode broken.

4. "I could use

those fold

tools," Dad said.

5. Rose liked the

stove rope.

SCHOOL-HOME CONNECTION Talk with your child about the ways the long *o* sound is spelled in the words on this page.

30

Extra Support
Gather Around • Lesson 4

Name _____

▶ **Read the selection. Then follow the directions.**

Even when you are looking for animal tracks, you might not be able to see them. Sometimes animals step on rocks or in other hard places. Then they don't leave tracks. Sometimes they step on leaves or plants. That makes their tracks harder to see.

▶ **Circle the sentence that tells the main idea of the selection, or what it is mostly about.**

1. It is not always easy to see animal tracks.
2. Sometimes animals step on rocks or in other hard places.
3. Sometimes animals step on leaves or plants.

Name _____

▶ **Trace the contraction under each set of underlined words.**

<u>They are</u>

1.  They're asking Mom and Dad for a dog.

<u>She had</u>

2.  She'd always wanted a horse.

<u>he would</u>

3. Bill said he'd like a hamster.

<u>we are</u>

4. They know we're hoping
for a kitten.

<u>They have</u>

5. They've

got lots of animals at the zoo.

SCHOOL-HOME CONNECTION Talk with your child
about the letters that the apostrophe stands for in
each contraction.

Extra Support
Gather Around • Lesson 4

▶ **Trace the word that matches the picture.
Cross out the other word.**

1. large small

2. bridge edge

3. center edge

4. germ giraffe

5. gill gem

 SCHOOL-HOME CONNECTION Have your
child tell why he or she traced each word. Then
have your child practice writing the letter *g* and
the letters *dge* in words.

 34

Extra Support
Gather Around • Lesson 5

Name _____

▶ **Trace the word that matches the clue.**
Cross out the other word.

1. You get this when you buy something.

range change

2. This could be in a back yard.

hedge ledge

3. This person wears a black robe.

smudge judge

4. This is part of a book.

page rage

5. This is a place for a pet bird.

age cage

SCHOOL-HOME CONNECTION Help your child
think of clues for some of the wrong answer
choices. Talk about the sound the letter *g* stands
for in the words.

Extra Support
Gather Around • Lesson 5

Name _____

▶ **Look at each picture and read the sentence. Trace the word that completes the sentence.**

1. Celeste was 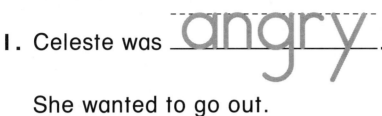 _____.

She wanted to go out.

2. It had been raining  all day.

3. Celeste asked, "Would it be  if I went out now?"

4. "I'm ,

Celeste. You must wait till the rain stops."

SCHOOL-HOME CONNECTION Read the sentences with your child. Talk about the meanings of the words your child traced.

37

Extra Support
Gather Around • Lesson 5

Name _____

▶ Trace the word that names the picture.
Cross out the other word.

1. rice mice

2. cage edge

3. hedge stage

4. dance space

5. badge page

 SCHOOL-HOME CONNECTION Ask your child to
read aloud the words he or she has traced. Then
have your child practice writing words with
c, *g*, and *dge*.

 38

Extra Support
Gather Around • Lesson 5

Name _____

▶ **Read the story and look at the pictures.**
Then circle the answers to the questions.

Madge's family left
in the morning.

They got to the camping
spot in the afternoon.

They set up camp.

They went fishing.

1. What happens in the beginning of the story?

Madge's family goes fishing.

Madge's family leaves to go camping.

2. What happens in the middle of the story?

Madge's family sets up camp.

Madge's family goes fishing.

3. What happens at the end of the story?

Madge's family gets to the camping spot.

Madge's family goes fishing.

SCHOOL-HOME CONNECTION Ask your child
what might happen next.

39

Extra Support
Gather Around • Lesson 5

▶ **Trace the word that completes the sentence. Cross out the other word.**

1. <u>They're They've</u>

going out in the rain.

2. <u>They've They're</u>

been splashing in the puddles.

3. Cecil said,

" <u>You're I've</u>

forgotten my umbrella."

4. Sally said <u>she'd we've</u>

be glad to share.

SCHOOL-HOME CONNECTION Ask your child to explain his or her answer choices. Then have your child practice writing words with 've, 'd, and 're.

40

Extra Support
Gather Around • Lesson 5

Name _____

► **Trace the word that matches the picture.**
  Cross out the other word.

1. tune cube

2. use mule

3. cute mule

4. rude tune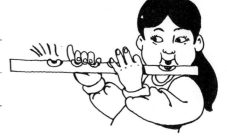

5. tube cute

 SCHOOL-HOME CONNECTION Have your child
tell why he or she traced each word. Then have
your child practice writing some of the words on
the page.

 42

Extra Support
Gather Around • Lesson 6

Name _____

▶ **Trace the word that completes the sentence. Cross out the other word.**

1. He needs a huge cube bed.

2. " Excuse
Rude me," she said. "May I help you?"

3. "I don't mean to be
mule rude ,"
he said.

4. "May I cute use
this bed to test it?" he asked.

SCHOOL-HOME CONNECTION Talk with your child about the vowel sound that *u-e* stands for in the traced words.

44

Name _____

▶ **Look at each picture and read the sentence. Trace the word that completes the sentence.**

1. The boy ___brought___ a flute.

2. He played a ___few___ tunes.

3. She ___read___ while he played.

4. Her ___head___ began to hurt.

SCHOOL-HOME CONNECTION Ask your child to practice writing the words *brought*, *few*, *head*, and *read* in original sentences.

45

Name _____

▶ **Trace the word that completes each sentence. Cross out the other word.**

1. Mule and Pig gave a tube huge party.

2. Mule made a cake grape for the party.

3. Pig cut tunes cubes of cheese.

4. Their friends got there at hive five.

SCHOOL-HOME CONNECTION Talk with your child about how the sentences go with the picture. Talk about the silent *e* in the words your child traced.

Name _____

► **Trace the word in each sentence that makes sense. Cross out the other word.**

1. Pig was skipping

   stopping along.

2. He gripped stopped

   to pick flowers.

3. He stepped missed

   over the mud.

4. He dropped dripped

   a flower.

SCHOOL-HOME CONNECTION Have your child
practice writing the words *skipping* and *stopped*.

47

Extra Support
Gather Around • Lesson 6

Name _____

▶ **Draw a line from the picture to the word that names it. Then trace the word.**

1.   head

2.   breakfast

3.   feather

4.   thread

5.   meadow

6.  bread

 SCHOOL-HOME CONNECTION Have your child practice writing the words *bread* and *feather*. Talk about the letters that stand for the short *e* sound in the words.

49

Extra Support
Gather Around • Lesson 7

Name _____

▶ **Trace the word that best completes each sentence. Cross out the other word.**

I. I like to

spread instead it.

2. I am

dread ready

for school.

3. What is the

weather sweat

like today?

4. It is a very

pleasant leather day.

SCHOOL-HOME CONNECTION Have your child practice writing the crossed-out words.

51

Extra Support
Gather Around • Lesson 7

Name _____

▶ **Look at each picture and read the sentence. Trace the word that completes the sentence.**

1. Ned's __parents__
tuck him in at night.

2. Ned sleeps eight __hours__
each night.

3. Ned likes to __carry__
his books in a backpack.

4. On Saturday afternoons,
Ned rides his

__bicycle__.

SCHOOL-HOME CONNECTION Read the sentences
with your child. Talk about how the sentences
describe the pictures.

52

Extra Support
Gather Around • Lesson 7

Name _____

▶ **Trace the word that completes each sentence. Cross out the other word.**

1. Ken's pet has no _____

pep   ten .

2. The _____den_____ _____vet_____ looks at the hen.

3. The feathers on her

head   had look bad.

4. This _____bed_____ _____hen_____

has to get more sleep!

5. Ken read spread

the vet's list.

SCHOOL-HOME CONNECTION Have your child practice reading the short *e* words on the page, paying attention to the letters that spell the sound in each word.

53

Extra Support
Gather Around • Lesson 7

Name _____

▶ **Read each story. Then circle the sentence that tells the main idea.**

I.   **Ben naps on the couch.**

People can nap in many different places.

Jen naps in a hammock.

Ben naps on the couch.

Deb naps in a chair.

Wes naps in his crib.

2.   **People like to do different things.**

Babies can not play baseball.

Jen likes baseball.

Ben likes to swim.

Deb is good at skating.

Wes tries to walk.

SCHOOL-HOME CONNECTION Have your child think of three details to support this main idea: People come from different places.

54

Name _____

▶ **Trace the word in each sentence that makes sense. Cross out the other word.**

1. Jed

patted planned

to help his mom.

2. Jed watched as his mom

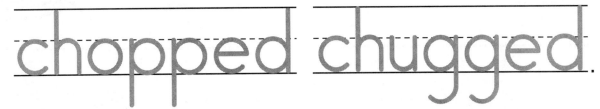

chopped chugged.

3. Jed put the

topping tapping

on the pie.

4. Mom is

hopping hugging

Jed.

 SCHOOL-HOME CONNECTION Discuss with your child the rule about doubling the final consonant of some words before adding -ing or -ed.

Extra Support
Gather Around • Lesson 7

▶ **Trace the word that has the same vowel sound as the word <u>tool</u>. Cross out the other word.**

1. school scale

2. fad food

3. pool pal

4. gas goose

5. men moon

SCHOOL-HOME CONNECTION Have your child say each pair of words and explain why he or she chose each answer. Talk about the letters that stand for the vowel sound in the traced words.

57

Extra Support
Gather Around • Lesson 8

© Harcourt

Name _____

► Trace the word that answers the
question or completes the sentence.
Cross out the other word.

1. What helps you eat?

tooth balloon

2. When do you eat lunch?

mood noon

3. What cleans your hair?

 shampoo bamboo

4. It's an ice house.

igloo school

5. This is a word to scare you.

soon boo

 SCHOOL-HOME CONNECTION Have your
child practice writing the words he or she
traced on this page.

 59

Extra Support
Gather Around • Lesson 8

Name _____

▶ **Look at each picture and read the sentence. Trace the word that completes the sentence.**

1. Joan shook the pot as the corn popped.

2. Her mom said, "Let's keep the fire hot."

3. Be careful!

4. Joan sat quietly and leaned against her mom as they read.

Extra Support
Gather Around • Lesson 8

Name _____

▶ **Trace the word that names the picture.**
Cross out the other word.

1. roof   tool

2. tooth   toad

3. throat   toast

4. cool   tool

5. soap   coat

SCHOOL-HOME CONNECTION Ask your child to point to all the words that have the same vowel sound as the word *fool.* Then have your child point to all the words that have the long *o* sound, as in *road.*   **61**

Extra Support
Gather Around • Lesson 8

Name _____

▶ **Look at the pictures and read the story.**
Then circle the correct answer to each question.

Goat set the table for her friends.

Goat made some food for them.

Oh, no! Goat dropped the food!

Goat used a broom.

Goat made some more food.

Goat's friends had a good time.

1. What happened in the beginning?

> **Goat's friends came over.**
>
> **Goat set the table.**

2. What happened in the middle?

> **Goat dropped the food.**
>
> **Goat's friends had a good time.**

3. What happened at the end?

> **Goat's friends had a good time.**
>
> **Goat used a broom.**

 SCHOOL-HOME CONNECTION Talk with your child about how the pictures help tell the story. Ask your child what might happen next.

 62

Name _____

▶ **Trace the word that goes with the picture. Cross out the other word.**

1. room loom

2. gloom broom

3. loot boot

4. root toot

5. zoom groom

6. hoot shoot

 SCHOOL-HOME CONNECTION Have your child explain his or her answer choices. Then have your child practice writing the letter combinations *oom* and *oot* in words.

 63

Answer Key

Extra Support
Answer Key

LEVEL 1 (Guess Who)

Page 9
1. cap
2. bag
3. ham

Page 11
1. ham
2. pan
3. cat
4. map
5. lamp

Page 12
1. up
2. down
3. got

Page 13
1. cat
2. Max
3. cap
4. bat
5. am

Page 14
1. 3; 1; 2
2. 2; 3; 1
3. 1; 3; 2

Page 15
Circled word:
1. at
2. ap
3. at
4. ap
5. at
6. ap
7. at
8. ap
9. at

Page 17
1. pan
2. cat
3. bat
4. mat
5. can
6. cap
7. bag
8. map

Page 19
1. "a" in hat
2. "a" in pan
3. "a" in cat
4. "a" in ham
5. "a" in bag
6. "a" in jam
7. "a" in fan
8. "a" in map
9. "a" in cap

Page 20
1. and
2. in
3. in
4. Yes
5. Oh

Page 21
1. hat
2. sand
3. bat
4. band
5. lamp
6. fan

Page 22
1. comes
2. pats
3. (*cat* not traced)
4. looks

Page 24
1. mitt; pin
2. lips; fin
3. pig; wig

Page 26
1. pig
2. zip
3. pin
4. crib
5. fish

Page 27
1. walk
2. They
3. make

Page 28
Circled words:
1. did
2. bib
3. hill
4. mitt

Page 29
1. Accept reasonable responses.

Page 30
1. Here's
2. What's
3. It's
4. Pat's

Page 32
1. tack
2. sack
3. kick

Page 34
Traced word:
1. sick
2. pick
3. sack
4. tack

Page 35
1. want
2. now
3. too
4. help
5. play

Page 36
1. tack
2. kick
3. sick
4. sack

Page 37
1. 2; 3; 1
2. 2; 1; 3

Page 38
1. I'll
2. You'll
3. we'll

Page 40
1. "o" in dog
2. "o" in top
3. "o" in box
4. "o" in mop
5. "o" in pot
6. "o" in cot

Page 42
1. top
2. box
3. log
4. cot
5. lock

Page 43
1. so
2. of
3. Don't

Page 44
1. o
2. i
3. i
4. o
5. i
6. o

Page 45
1. looked
2. looking
3. picked
4. picking

Page 47
1. tall
2. hall
3. call
4. ball

Page 49
Cut-out word:
1. fall
2. ball
3. tall
4. hall

Page 50
1. buy
2. Where
3. that
4. very

Page 51
1. hall
2. rock
3. lick
4. fall
5. pill

Page 52
1. fresh snow figure
2. snow figure beginning to melt
3. melted snow figure

Page 53
1. isn't
2. don't
3. aren't
4. Didn't

LEVEL 2 (Catch a Dream)

Page 3
Circled word:
1. neck
2. leg
4. ten
6. net
8. men
9. hen
10. vest
12. fence

Page 5
1. tent
2. nest
3. belt
4. web
5. pen
6. hen
7. bell
8. sled

Page 6
1. with; her
2. was
3. said
4. every day

Page 7
1. jet
2. doll
3. pond
4. belt
5. cot
6. wet
7. fox
8. mend

Page 8
1. picture of playground
2. picture of bedroom

Page 9
1. sp
2. sn
3. sl
4. st
5. sp
6. sk

Page 11
1. thumb
2. thirty
3. teeth
4. thorn
5. moth
6. path
7. math
8. bath

Page 13
1. cloth
2. thick
3. thin
4. broth

Page 14
1. She; friends
2. could; use
3. put
4. new

Page 15
1. fist; crib
2. belt; desk
3. melt; vest
4. tent; dent
5. twin; film

Page 16
1. nest, best
2. tent, dent

Page 18
1. bus
2. mug
3. sun
4. tub
5. duck
6. bug
7. nut
8. puppy

Page 20
1. pup; cup
2. sun; run
3. drum; crumb
4. jump; hump
5. plus; bus

Page 21
1. Your; out
2. says; he
3. gives; night
4. People; when

Page 22
1. leg
2. hug
3. truck
4. men

Page 23
1. frog; frame
2. drum; dress
3. pretzel; prince
4. tricycle; trick
5. grass; grapes

Page 25
1. king
2. sing
3. wing
4. string
5. swing
6. ring
7. hang
8. sting

Page 27
1. sing
2. fang
3. ring
4. string
5. king

Page 28
1. two
2. grows; eat
3. from
4. gone; or

Page 29
1. sled
2. trap
3. stand
4. stamp
5. sing

Page 30
1. tent
2. dog
4. cats
5. log

Page 31
1. He's
2. isn't
3. He'll
4. can't
5. They'll

Page 33
1. thorn; corn
2. fork; stork
3. snore; store
4. port; short
5. horn; torn

Page 35
1. corn
2. sport
3. stork
4. horn
5. thorn
6. shorts

Page 36
1. need; be
2. try; good
3. our; time
4. saw; right

Page 37
1. for
2. cord
3. torn
4. horn
5. corn

Page 38
1. Dennis
2. Mom; Dad

Page 39
1. softball
2. backpack
3. sunset
4. bathtub
5. popcorn

Page 41
1. dish
2. shoe
3. ship
4. shell
5. brush
6. shack
7. shark
8. shelf

Page 43
1. dish; brush
2. shell; shack
3. mash; cash
4. shorts; crush

Page 44
1. some
2. How; many
3. hide; away
4. Their; funny

Page 45
1. ship
2. dish
3. shut
4. cash
5. mash

Page 46
1. fish
2. Fins
3. plants

Page 47
1. truck
2. frog
3. swing
4. dress
5. sled
6. swim

LEVEL 3
(Here and There)

Page 3
1. trace
2. cross out
3. trace
4. trace
5. trace
6. trace
7. trace
8. cross out
9. trace

Page 5
1. chin
2. chick
3. patch
4. catch
5. pitch

Page 6
1. live
2. Soon
3. turns
4. fly

Page 7
1. pitch
2. such
3. dash
4. fetch

Page 8
1. fl
2. sl
3. cl
4. pl
5. cl
6. fl
7. pl
8. cl
9. sl

Page 10
1. car
2. arm
3. barn
4. card
5. bar

Page 12
1. car
2. barn
3. jar
4. star
5. bar

Page 13
1. house
2. city
3. there
4. take

Page 14
1. car
2. start
3. hard
4. farm
5. far

Page 15
1. picture of barn
2. picture of school

Page 16
1. jumped
2. jumps
3. jumping
4. walking
5. walks

Page 18
1. qu
2. wh
3. qu
4. wh
5. wh
6. wh
7. qu
8. qu

Page 20
1. quilt
2. quack
3. quiz
4. when
5. whip

Page 21
1. family
2. read
3. grew
4. writing

Page 22
1. When
2. quit
3. Which
4. this
5. quick

Page 23
Circled character:
1. alligator in party hat
Checked characters:
1. alligator in apron
2. turtle in cap

Page 24
1. clam
2. flag
3. plug
4. sled
5. clock

Page 26
1. girl
2. fern
3. bird
4. turn
5. curb

Page 28
1. yes
2. yes
3. no
4. yes
5. yes

Page 29
1. way
2. were
3. full
4. find

Page 30
1. birds
2. duck
3. third
4. met
5. her

Page 31
1. picture of snow falling
2. picture of busy city

Page 32
1. called
2. calling
3. rings
4. ringing
5. picks

Page 34
1. trace
2. cross out
3. trace
4. trace
5. trace
6. cross out
7. trace
8. cross out
9. trace

Page 36
1. little
2. pickle
3. turtle
4. apple
5. candle

Page 37
1. school
2. together
3. talk
4. each

Page 38
1. tickle
2. giggle
3. puddle

Page 39
1. small
2. smaller
3. smallest
4. fastest

Page 41
1. coat
2. boat
3. bowl
4. snow
5. road
6. bow
7. soap
8. goat

Page 43
1. bow
2. toad
3. goat
4. bowl
5. coat

Page 44
1. Who
2. Would
3. made
4. kind

Page 45
1. goat
2. boat
3. float
4. mop
5. hot

Page 46
1. dog wearing suit
2. wolf

Page 47
1. likes
2. rowed
3. rowing
4. rows
5. swims

LEVEL 4 *(Time Together)*

Page 9
1. she
2. bee
3. sleep
4. eat
5. leap
6. peach

Page 11
1. beads; red beads
2. beets; purple beets
3. beak; beak should be colored
4. seal; seal should be colored

Page 12
1. know
2. moved
3. room
4. write

Page 13
1. Dean
2. bees
3. jeans
4. bowl
5. coat
6. read

Page 14
1. h; i; j; k
2. p; q; r; s
3. b; d; f; g
4. r; t; v; x
5. l; n; o; q

Page 15
1. She's
2. Doesn't
3. She'll
4. He's

Page 17
1. lake
2. grapes
3. save
4. Jane's
5. race

Page 19
1. lake
2. game
3. face
4. gate
5. vase

Page 20
1. country
2. Earth
3. world
4. town

Page 21
Traced word:
1. base
2. pane
3. mate
4. cane
5. tape
Circled word:
1. bat
2. pan
3. mat
4. can
5. tap

Page 22
Things That Move:
1. truck
2. plane
3. car
4. bus
Things That Do Not Move:
1. house
2. hill
3. pond
4. cave

Page 23
1. named
2. racing

Page 25
1. penny
2. sandy
3. happy
4. soapy
5. sixty
6. cherry

Page 27
1. bunny
2. buggy
3. happy
4. dirty
5. hilly

Page 28
1. hold
2. different
3. water
4. years

Page 29
1. party
2. cherry
3. hurry
4. thin
5. very

Page 30
Circled lists:
1. Animals in the Water
2. Animals on the Land

Page 31
1. hurried
2. flies
3. hurries
4. berries
5. tried

Page 33
1. time
2. vine
3. rise
4. bike
5. pine

Page 35
1. hive
2. like
3. ride
4. bride
5. white

Page 36
1. cook
2. listen
3. picture
4. young

Extra Support
Answer Key

Page 37
1. bite
2. fin
3. dime
4. kit
5. file

Page 38
1. ball; call; doll
2. rag; sag; tag
3. lap; map; nap

Page 39
1. She's
2. didn't
3. They'll
4. She'll

Page 41
1. city
2. cent
3. pencil
4. prince
5. dance
6. space

Page 43
1. race
2. face
3. nice
4. dance
5. twice

Page 44
1. always
2. even
3. pretty
4. sound

Page 45
1. lace
2. mice
3. trace
4. price
5. space

Page 46
1. ride
2. price
3. bride
4. rice
5. tide

Page 48
1. crown
2. bow
3. cloud
4. hour
5. tower

Page 50
1. pound
2. town
3. ground
4. found
5. flowers

Page 51
1. eight
2. Dr.
3. busy
4. any

Page 52
1. clown
2. pouch
3. towel
4. scout
5. power

Page 53
Circled lists:
1. Words About Color
2. Words About Feelings

Page 54
1. frown
2. gown
3. round
4. ground
5. clown

Page 56
1. sky
2. fly
3. cry
4. pie
5. fries
6. tie

Page 58
1. my
2. tie
3. why
4. by
5. pie

Page 59
1. opened
2. Hello
3. high
4. love

Page 60
1. tie
2. tried
3. tricky
4. worry
5. my

Page 61
Circled words:
1. Jan; Kim; Liz; Max
2. Ed; Fran; Gil; Hal
3. Pat; Sam; Tim; Will

Page 62
1. He's
2. doesn't
3. She'll
4. She's

Page 64
1. bone
2. robe
3. rose
4. pole
5. home

Page 66
1. throne
2. spoke
3. hopes
4. nose
5. close

Page 67
1. field
2. twelve
3. touch
4. change

Page 68
1. joke
2. hop
3. bone
4. rod
5. pose

Page 69
1. black
2. fly
3. flowers
4. flock

LEVEL 5 (Gather Around)

Page 3
1. night
2. light
3. high
4. bright
5. tight

Page 5
1. high
2. night
3. bright
4. light
5. sigh

A6

Page 6
1. thought
2. afraid
3. learn
4. Nothing
5. join

Page 7
1. boat
2. tight
3. high
4. beach
5. night

Page 8
1. man taking off coat

Page 9
1. liked
2. raced
3. tasting
4. chasing
5. decided

Page 11
1. snail
2. paint
3. tray
4. stain
5. hay

Page 13
1. train
2. sail
3. tail
4. play
5. gray

Page 14
1. caught
2. hurried
3. near
4. cold
5. sure

Page 15
1. make
2. clay
3. painted
4. cake
5. plate

Page 16
1. skating
2. racing
3. chasing
4. waved
5. taped

Page 18
1. mind
2. wild
3. child
4. behind
5. find

Page 20
1. mind
2. child
3. wild
4. wind
5. behind

Page 21
1. during
2. ready
3. Both
4. ready

Page 22
1. kite
2. slide
3. wind
4. child
5. smile

Page 23
Circled response:
2. Wild animals have to find food for themselves.

Page 24
1. hitting
2. slammed
3. dropped
4. skidded
5. clapping

Page 26
1. Most
2. told
3. cold
4. hold
5. Hello

Page 28
1. hold
2. post
3. old
4. hello
5. fold

Page 29
1. pulls
2. nature
3. floor
4. clues
5. piece
6. detective

Page 30
1. Most
2. hole
3. broken
4. those
5. stove

Page 31
Circled response:
1. It is not always easy to see animal tracks.

Page 32
1. They're
2. She'd
3. he'd
4. we're
5. They've

Page 34
1. large
2. bridge
3. edge
4. giraffe
5. gem

Page 36
1. change
2. hedge
3. judge
4. page
5. cage

Page 37
1. angry
2. nearly
3. okay
4. sorry

Page 38
1. mice
2. cage
3. stage
4. dance
5. badge

Page 39
1. Madge's family leaves to go fishing.
2. Madge's family sets up camp.
3. Madge's family goes fishing.

Extra Support
Answer Key

Page 40
1. They're
2. They've
3. I've
4. she'd

Page 42
1. cube
2. mule
3. cute
4. tune
5. tube

Page 44
1. huge
2. Excuse
3. rude
4. use

Page 45
1. brought
2. few
3. read
4. head

Page 46
1. huge
2. cake
3. cubes
4. five

Page 47
1. skipping
2. stopped
3. stepped
4. dropped

Page 49
1. feather
2. thread
3. head
4. bread
5. meadow
6. breakfast

Page 51
1. spread
2. ready
3. weather
4. pleasant

Page 52
1. parents
2. hours
3. carry
4. bicycle

Page 53
1. pep
2. vet
3. head
4. hen
5. read

Page 54
1. People nap in many different places.
2. People like to do different things.

Page 55
1. planned
2. chopped
3. topping
4. hugging

Page 57
1. school
2. food
3. pool
4. goose
5. moon

Page 59
1. tooth
2. noon
3. shampoo
4. igloo
5. boo

Page 60
1. shook
2. fire
3. careful
4. quietly

Page 61
1. roof
2. tooth
3. toast
4. tool
5. soap

Page 62
1. Goat set the table.
2. Goat dropped the food.
3. Goat's friends had a good time.

Page 63
1. room
2. broom
3. boot
4. root
5. groom
6. shoot

Extra Support
Answer Key